CORNELIA GUEST'S
SIMPLE
PLEASURES

My favorite picture of all time! Madonna, my little devil, I just adore her.

*Soba Salad. I love playing around
with different types of noodles.
These Bee dishes are so old I only
use them for special occasions.
Recipe on page 94.*

The Topiary Garden.
Russell Page designed it.

Menu
June 7, 2011
Dinner
Tempeh Pot Pie
Vegetable Carpaccio
Grilled Bread
Cucumber Cooler
Domaines OTT Rosé

Cornelia Guest Cookies with my fox cups. My father never liked to use them as his fingers were too big to fit in the handles! I loved them when I was little.

Me, Nelson, and
Mickie in the Rose Garden.

CORNELIA GUEST'S
SIMPLE
PLEASURES

HEALTHY SEASONAL COOKING AND EASY ENTERTAINING

with

DIANE REVERAND

WEINSTEIN
BOOKS

Also by Cornelia Guest

The Debutante's Guide to Life
with Carol McD. Wallace

Cover photograph © 2012 Bruce Weber
Food photographs © 2012 Matthew Klein
Photo, page 12 © 2012 Christina Gerry
Illustrations © 2012 Nina Duran
Photos page 248 © 2012 Nina Duran

Printed in China.

For more information address
Weinstein Books
387 Park Avenue South, 12th Floor,
New York, NY 10016

ISBN: 978-1-60286-162-6 (hardcover)
ISBN: 978-1-60286-168-8 (e-book)

First Edition
10 9 8 7 6 5 4 3 2 1

CREATIVE DIRECTOR J-C Suarès
ART DIRECTOR Kathleen Gates
ILLUSTRATOR Nina Duran

INTERIOR PHOTOS Matthew Klein
ASSISTANT Tom Cinko
FOOD STYLIST Charlotte Omnes
ASSISTANT FOOD STYLIST Bashirah Connor

To Nelson,
xo
Cornelia

I keep some of my utensils in this old copper pot I found at a flea market in Paris.

ACKNOWLEDGMENTS

Mark Badgley
Kari Breglia
Bobbi Brown
Nan Bush
Maureen Case
Teal Cannaday
Piotr Cesarski
Debra Cindrich
Tom Cinko
Bashirah Connor
Leonardo Corleto
Russ Cutler
John Demsey
Carolyn Depalma
Jeff DePeron
Nina Duran
Andrew Egan
Pauline Esposito
Jack Estevinto
Tim Evans
Alexandra Fahrni
Douglas Friedman
Dr. Michael Galitzer
Oz Garcia

Kathleen Gates
Karen Giberson
Ali Gimson
Tomaz Golombos
Addie Grant
Chef Michael Guerrieri
Nelson Guest
Bear Guest
Giorgio Guidotti
Ricki Gurtman
Judy Hottensen
Kirpal
Matthew Klein
Robin Lacker
Jenna LaSpina
Peri Lyons
Missy Malkin
Armando Mania
Marchesa
Marko Matijas
Lisa Merkel
James Mischka
Charlotte Omnes
Ruth Ordanza

Barbara Oxer
Mitchell Parness
David Peak
Chef Tanya Petrovna
Nakia Ray
Diane Reverand
Matthew Richards
Matthew Roberts
Jeanette Shaheen
Colin Shanley
Davina Shinewell
Sol Slotnik
Joe Spellman
J. C. Suares
Florentina Tanase
Rodica Tanase
Joanna Vargas
David Vigliano
Dr. Surinder Wadyal
Deborah Watson
Bruce Weber
Harvey Weinstein

CONTENTS

I have two lantana trees
in the rose garden,
hummingbirds love them.

A Note from the Author

Simple Pleasures is a lifestyle—an unpretentious way to live. It gives you the best of everything. For me, it's all about simplicity. That's what this book is about: natural elegance, wholesome eating, and effortless entertaining. Nobody likes pretension. Elaborate foods and fussy parties are no longer. Food, flowers, plates, glasses, you name it, I keep things as close to their original state as possible.

Elegance comes from an attitude that is confident, kind, and open to everything. I grew up surrounded by extraordinary people and learned so much from them— ways of doing things that have enhanced my life. I never forget that charm is the most important part of elegance.

One of my favorite passions is animals, which is why I believe in cruelty-free eating. I do not eat foods that use animal products, but I am not a vegan fanatic. *Simple Pleasures* will show you that fresh vegetables, beans, and grains are delicious, affordable, and easy to make. You don't have to be vegan to enjoy the wonderful seasonal recipes in this book. Your friends and family probably won't miss the meat when you serve scrumptious, satisfying food that does not hurt animals. There are lots of health benefits from eating a plant-based diet. To start, you will look and feel better. If you are "almost" vegan or vegetarian, these recipes might inspire you to be more so. If you are not even close, well, okay, try the recipes as side dishes so that you and your family will eat more veggies.

Entertaining should be fun, relaxing, a way to fill our lives with family, friends, and wonderful memories. It should never feel like torture. Trust me. Entertaining is in my blood. I know how to make it easy. I have a few sacred rules that will make your entertaining effortless, stress-free, and most importantly, fun for all.

Whether it's a party for two, twenty, or two hundred, I keep it simple. If I get crazy, none of it is fun, and I don't enjoy my own party. I'll pass along my secrets to effortless entertaining that will boost your confidence and make having friends over a pleasure.

I hope *Simple Pleasures* helps you discover your passion and love for Mother Nature and all her wonderful gifts.

Cornelia Guest
JULY 2011

PART 1

SIMPLE PLEASURES

I love birds and try to have lots of birdhouses. I love seeing who
comes back year after year. I feed everyone all year long.

CHAPTER 1
Easy Elegance

For me, style is a way of living. It's so much more than how you look. Style is an attitude. It's about making sure that your whole life works. I have been lucky to have wonderful teachers. C. Z. Guest, my mother, had an iconic sense of style. She always knew what was distinctive and appropriate. It didn't matter if it was how to dress, manners, decorating the house, making gardens, planning parties—her instincts were always perfect.

My first riding instructor, Katie Monahan Prudent, taught me discipline. There was no sleeping in for me. I had my horses to take care of and hours of riding without stirrups to get ready for shows. I had determination, but her strict sense of discipline has carried over from riding to how I live my life. I couldn't have had a better style mentor than Halston, who was so kind and generous to me. I had good times with Andy Warhol, who taught me that anyone or anything is fascinating.

Great style begins with being comfortable in your own skin. Style means being natural, having the relaxed graciousness that comes from being confident, kind, and open to everyone and everything. Pretension, excess, and uptightness are my biggest pet peeves. In *Simple Pleasures*, I'd like to show you a way of living, the easy elegance I learned from my family and our illustrious friends. I want to return to those basic values and show you an affordable and simple way to live with style. Style has so many elements—an inviting and comfortable house, a beautiful table whether or not you have family

Tulips in old polo trophies
out by the pool.

heirlooms, delicious, unfussy food, good manners, and understatement all contribute to simple elegance accessible to anyone.

As elegant as my parents were, they were country people at heart. They loved their horses and their dogs, and to be at home at our house, Templeton. My father, Winston Guest, had teatime every day at 5 P.M. I remember him smoking his cigar, surrounded by our Jack Russells. I must have had ten of them. My original Jack Russell, named Jack, and his wife, Tootsie, had puppies, and so on, and so on, and so on. We kept them all!

I grew up watching my parents entertain—formal dinners, poolside cocktails, a constant stream of guests. Our house was always filled with extraordinary people, from the Duke and Duchess of Windsor to Rudolf Nureyev, from Truman Capote to Yves Saint Laurent. I was always brought down to see the adults before dinner. I was taught to curtsy, so I curtsied to everyone, and if I didn't I would get a swift whack on my rear from my mother or my beloved Mademoiselle, whom I named Maze.

I was like a sponge. What I saw, what I heard, and what I learned from all those wonderful people made me who I am today. I was fascinated by the archaeologist Iris Cornelia Love. I loved that she and I shared the same name and that she discovered the Garden of Aphrodite. All I wanted to talk about was her digs, and I dreamed of digging with her one day.

Templeton, my family's home where I now live, is beautiful. We shot the photographs for *Simple Pleasures* there, because so much of who I am and how I live comes from Templeton, where I learned from the best. I work in the gardens, play with my dogs, bake cookies for my business, Cornelia Guest Cookies, and invite my friends over to eat food mostly grown in my garden. The house was decorated more than thirty years ago. The rooms are cluttered with photos and beautiful things that bring back so many memories.

The rugs are worn, faded chintz and vibrant colors are everywhere, the faux-marble finishes are chipped, and family portraits by John Singer Sargent, Dalí, and Andy Warhol hang on the walls. The house has a classic, old-guard look that never goes out of style. It is the flip side of the minimalism that is now so in vogue. Templeton is cheerful, colorful, and comfortable. For me, the house embodies the feeling of a well-lived life.

I've always been a homebody, like my parents, happiest at Templeton. I returned whenever life got crazy. I came home for good in 1995 when my mother was diagnosed with cancer. She always said, "Anybody can go off, the trick is coming back."

My mother, a maverick herself, had supported my move to Hollywood to pursue an acting career. She left her very proper family in Boston for the same reason and ended up onstage at the Ziegfeld Follies. Years later, she broke the rules again by working. After a riding accident laid her up, she began to write a gardening column that eventually was syndicated in 350 newspapers. She developed gardening products and fragrances and designed a line of cashmere sweaters for Adolfo. She was a trendsetter. None of her friends were doing anything like that.

When I made my debut, my mother's advice to me was "Be polite, meet everybody, and have a wonderful life." I took her advice to heart. I enjoyed life in New York as a debutante. I was lucky enough to have three de facto fairy godfathers, Andy Warhol, Halston, and Scavullo. Andy Warhol was a close friend, a genius, who taught me not to lose a sense of wonder and to believe that you can get wisdom anywhere, from every possible place.

Halston taught me how to walk in a dress on a makeshift runway in his studio. One day he told me I walked like an elephant. He put me in a dress with a pair of high-heeled—five inches—shoes that laced up my ankles. He said in his booming voice, "Walk!"

I teetered halfway up the runway.

He slammed down a book with a bang and said, "Walk properly." He got up and demonstrated what he had in mind. "Now walk," he commanded.

And walk I did. I knew enough to avoid the wrath of Halston.

Then he said the immortal words, "Beauty knows no pain."

I cannot tell you how many fashion disasters he saved me from.

Scavullo, the renowned photographer, came to watch me in horse shows. He was a great support to me after my father died when I was seventeen. One day I had a terrible fall right in front of him. I was taught if you could get up, you'd better. I jumped up and turned around, and there was Francesco sweating and white as a ghost with a look of horror on his face. The paramedics ran right past me and straight to him. And, boy, did he ever give me hell for almost giving him a heart attack.

The eighties were a great time to be a party girl. The scenes at Studio 54, Xenon, and Regine's kept me out every night. The time came when I wanted to be someone different for a while. I had to do more than go to parties and ride my horses. I needed a purpose. So I went to Hollywood.

After five years of studying out West and getting some bit parts, I was drawn back to Templeton.

I began to read all I could about health when my mother was first diagnosed with breast cancer. Everything I read seemed to point me toward a simple equation: Food = Health. I read *The China Study, Farm Sanctuary* by

Gene Bauer, books by Dr. Dean Ornish, Dr. Neal Barnard, and many more. I realized the untested chemicals used in processed foods and the residue of pesticides and many fertilizers had to be hurting us. I began to notice that my animals were developing lumps and bumps that I don't remember them having when I was growing up. I knew then that it was time to make some changes.

Notes from My Friends

Dr. Richard Palmquist is an angel of animals. I had just adopted a Great Pyrenees from Gentle Giants Rescue. It was love at first sight. I named him Bear. He was covered in hot spots, and I was desperate for a great vet. A friend had told me about Dr. Palmquist, so off we went. Poor Bear was absolutely terrified. When I took him to Dr. Palmquist to deal with his skin condition, he put himself in the corner of the exam room, and all 150 pounds of him were shaking like a leaf. He had already been given away twice, and I think he thought I was going to do the same.

"Dr. P" came in, ignored me, and sat down right next to Bear. He scratched his ears, kissed his nose. Bear relaxed, and I realized we were at the right place and what an incredibly special person Dr. P was.

Bear and I spent a lot of time there, and Bear's health just got better and better. Dr. P uses a lot of homeopathy, but when he needs to will use traditional medicine. He lives and practices in Los Angeles and, lucky for me, is just a phone call away. I have asked him to talk about the best ways for us to protect our beloved critters.

Your Pets Need to Be Protected from Toxins, Too

When people begin to use natural medicine and products, their health improves and they learn new and healthier ways of living. In the process, they spread the good news to others. Now more than ever we are seeing a massive movement to healthier, gentler, and more cooperative lifestyles, and that includes how we care for our pets.

Toxins of all sorts damage our bodies and those of our pets. Bodies react by creating the various diseases we see each day in our clinics. Toxic food additives and environmental or medical toxins lead our bodies to expend energy to repair damage and eliminate those biologically unfriendly substances.

When it comes to our pets, health and happiness begins with a safe space and proper nutrition. Our website has some simple tips about pet health and the use of integrative medicine for animals: *www.lovapet.com/tips.nxg/#aspects*

RICHARD PALMQUIST, DVM
Author of Releasing Your Pet's Hidden Health Potential *and Chief of Integrative Health Services at Centinela Animal Hospital, Inglewood, California*

My concern about what I ate started even before all my reading and research. When I was twelve, I told my parents I would never eat another animal again. I have always loved critters great and small. I would rescue anything I could get my hands on. I brought home snakes, gerbils, turtles, fish, bunnies, and birds. I even rescued a pig. I think that's where my veganism all started. I never understood how my furry friends were any different from the animals we were eating, and I could not imagine eating one of them. That lasted until my doctor said I needed animal proteins to grow up big and strong. So meat became part of my diet again.

Notes from My Friends

Dan Mathews, the senior vice-president of campaigns at PETA, has uncanny intelligence about people and animals. He knows when to push and when not to. He knows how to get things done. The legislation protecting animals that he has accomplished is amazing. His love and compassion for animals is very deep. I am constantly in awe of him. I couldn't think of a better person to discuss cruelty to animals and other reasons why people choose to drop meat from their diets.

PETA Wants You to Think Before You Eat

PETA, which has more than two million members worldwide, recognizes that people have the right to eat whatever they want. We just want people to make informed decisions. That's why we conduct undercover video investigations in factory farms and slaughterhouses to show consumers that even the measly laws that exist to protect cows and pigs and chickens are routinely violated. Very few people—although there are some—want to hurt animals. PETA has emboldened consumers to fight animal cruelty with their forks by trying a vegan diet and not giving money to the violent meat and dairy industries.

Aside from animal cruelty issues, many people decide to shun meat because they want to avoid heart disease, cancer, and obesity. That's why PETA showcases so many fit vegan celebrities in their campaigns.

Others decide to drop meat from their diet after learning how the meat trade is the number one polluter on the planet: farmed animals and all the smelly transport trucks are the number one cause of greenhouse gas emissions. Chemicals and waste from factory farms also choke the life out of beautiful rivers and bays. They say the Chesapeake Bay looked like the Caribbean a hundred years ago—before decades of being fouled by runoff from all the huge chicken farms in Delaware and Maryland. PETA goes to great lengths to give people this food for thought so they can make up their own minds on what to put in their mouths. You can read more at *PETA.org.*

DAN MATHEWS
*Senior Vice-President of
Campaigns, PETA*

As I grew up, I realized I never felt great the days after I ate meat. I was a carnivore and loved a big, fatty steak with a big bone, but my body didn't. I ate less meat and lots of fish, but my mercury levels got very high. I gave up stinky cheeses, which I loved, and unless I saw the hen laying the egg, I would pass.

The reading I was doing when I came home supported my childhood intuition. I read about how the beautiful creatures we were eating led the most tortured, hideous lives imaginable. I had no idea this level of cruelty existed, and I wanted no part of it.

I was ready for a major change in my life. I have always been one to jump right in and a firm believer in "no time like the present." I threw myself into the vegan world. I was in awe of all the wonderfully delicious things I could eat that I had no idea about. Kale and quinoa never appeared on my parents' table. I felt that I had so much more energy, and I felt more level. My skin just glowed. I could tell my new way of eating was working, because I was getting compliments on how I looked from everyone. I was thrilled—and who doesn't love a compliment?

After six months on a vegan diet, I felt much happier, lighter, and I wasn't so impatient. I believe that the fear and anger of animals is transferred to us through their meat. By removing animal products from my diet, I'm healthier than I have ever been, and there is the added benefit of a bit of weight loss. I have become a convert and want to encourage healthy, wholesome eating. I know not all your friends are ready to become vegan. It is not my intention to alienate you by being too obsessive, but it is my intent to ask you to think and to inspire you and show you a different way.

Notes from My Friends

Alexandra Fahrni, my Pilates teacher, changed my body. She understands how emotions are held in the body and block the flow of energy. I see exercise differently now. I move to get the energy flowing.

Flow

Today, everything is so fast. Homes are now wired for quick, unencumbered access to a world of information. The global flow of ideas goes on 24/7. Everything is highly charged and moves with the speed of light.

That electric energy is the same as the vital force that flows through us, a life force that makes things move. Energy that moves freely in our bodies allows abstract thought and creativity. But substance, like our bodies, is denser than energy. Just as we have to re-charge our laptops and phones and clear our e-mails, we have to recharge our bodies to sweep away the blockages. What we eat, think, and love affects how the life force moves in our body. The flow of our energy can get blocked. The wrong

food, negativity, and passions can make us feel heavy, slow, and plodding. For some, the suffering of animals is trans-mitted in the food we eat and throws off the body's balance.

The way we move indicates how the energy is flowing. We want to fly, not plod, to move like light. Movement is the expression of our body's responses to the flow of energy within us and outside us, the physical manifestation of what we give and what we get.

ALEXANDRA FAHRNI

We all have a great capacity for change, but only for the right reasons. You must have a firm belief, a passion for the change you are making, otherwise it simply will not work. For me, these changes are right. I never feel deprived or that I'm missing something. In fact, just the opposite is true. I learn something new every day, and the opportunities are endless. Every time I turn on the TV, I hear about the recall of beef, eggs, and milk because of bacteria. It all starts in factory farms where animals are kept and bred. On the other hand, whenever I go to a farmers' market, I find such a huge selection with many new varieties of vegetables. Easy access to great produce makes me want to experiment in the kitchen.

I am now about to make another major transition in my life. Putting Templeton on the market is the most liberating thing I have ever done. There are so many ghosts in that house. That part of my life is over, and the world has changed. I want my own house and my own garden. I have made Templeton as much my own as I could, but the house has a built-in level of formality. In some sense, I have always felt like a visitor. I want to build a place of my own with enough land for me to have a small organic farm and to be able to adopt all the animals I can fit.

I decided to write *Simple Pleasures* to share what I know about relaxed elegance, entertaining with ease, and my own passion for eating in the most healthful way possible, which for me is a vegan diet.

CHAPTER 2

Wholesome Eating

Not all of you are ready to take the big leap and drop all animal products from your diet cold turkey, the way I did. Some of you might want to ease into giving cruelty-free eating a try. Others might realize that you and your family are not eating enough vegetables and know the change would be good for everyone. You are not alone. Only a quarter of Americans eat at least three servings of vegetables a day—and that includes potatoes. Since the current guidelines recommend a minimum of four daily servings of vegetables for women and five for men and two to four servings of fruit, we are far off the mark in our eating habits. Most of us Americans need to add more vegetables and fruits to our diet.

I would like to change the way you think about food. Instead of always building a menu around meat, poultry, fish, and eggs, you'll see how easy it is to make satisfying, yummy dishes from vegetables, grains, legumes, and fruits. My intention is to take the crunch out of granola and to inspire you to try a different way of cooking.

All the interest in farmers' markets and eating locally grown food has become a trend. "Locavores" are taking the next step and are becoming "vegavores," who love vegetables. Chefs all over the country are rising to the challenge and experimenting with vegetarian cuisine. "Meatless Mondays" have become popular in the best restaurants. I hope my delicious and flavor-packed recipes in *Simple Pleasures* will inspire you to eat more wholesome, fresh food. You can make small adjustments to eat well

Radishes straight from the dirt. I love to wash them off in the garden and eat them ASAP when they are still warm from the ground.

and to take advantage of the fresh produce that is available each season. That is why I have done this book by seasons—to make it simple.

There is so much to say about wholesome eating that it's impossible for me to cover all the issues and recommendations in a single chapter. Instead, I am giving you a quick look at what mattered to me as I became more focused on

Notes from My Friends

After my mother died, I gained thirty-five pounds. I went on a strict regimen and lost the weight, but my body still wasn't right. My emotions were overwhelming. My body had stopped. I went to a doctor who gave me some supplements that made me so sick I couldn't get out of bed. I had always been so active, and now I couldn't walk around the block. I felt my body had short-circuited. I was a mess—and terrified!

My friend Suzanne Somers recommended Dr. Michael Galitzer, who practices energy medicine and homeopathy. He saved my life. He taught me how the mind affects the body and how the organs work. I asked him to help me fill you in on some of the most important nutritional and environmental issues that affect your well-being. Now that you are thinking about eating in the most healthful way, I asked him to give you guidelines about the foods you should steer clear of.

Dr. Michael Galitzer's Top Ten Foods to Avoid

1. Red meat Meat contains hormones and antibiotics that impair health. If you remain a carnivore, try to stick to grass-fed and hormone-free meat. The same goes for chicken and other poultry.

2. Pork and processed meats Pork has been associated with viruses, and the additives in processed meat can be harmful.

3. Peanuts contain a mold called aflatoxin that has been associated with cancer. Many people are allergic to them.

4. Dairy Many people are sensitive to cow's milk or have a casein allergy. Casein, a protein in milk, can produce a reaction that includes a runny nose, itchy skin, or swollen lips.

5. Sugar and artificial sweeteners Sugar weakens the immune system. Artificial sweeteners have been associated with weight gain and can be harmful to brain cells.

6. Alcohol is a toxin and a depressant.

7. Trans-fatty acids, vegetable oils, and fried foods are associated with increased risk of cardiovascular disease.

8. Carbonated soft drinks are very acidic, and non-diet soft drinks have ten tablespoons of sugar in twelve ounces.

9. Tuna and swordfish have a high mercury content. Mercury is harmful to the hormonal and immune systems.

10. Allergic foods Eight foods are responsible for 90 percent of food allergy reactions: milk, eggs, peanuts, tree nuts (cashews, walnuts, and almonds), corn, shellfish, soy, and wheat. Eating these foods can cause immune reactions that have to be neutralized by the liver and the adrenal hormones, which can contribute to adrenal fatigue.

MICHAEL GALITZER, M.D.

what to eat. Since I am not a doctor or a health professional, I have asked my friends, experts in their fields, to cover subjects that I think are important. They help me keep my body, mind, and spirit in the best shape possible. I want to pass on the advice they have given me in their own words. Their insights and knowledge are always a huge help and inspiration to me.

Last year as my birthday present I asked my friends to give me one meatless day a week, or if that was too much, once a month. Most are still doing it, and are surprised at how they are making different choices with their food across the board. We become accustomed to what we eat. My friends are finding that eating differently has changed their taste buds. Junk food and meat have lost their appeal. They have found that reducing their weekly intake of animal products one thing at a time works. You might stop eating bacon, butter, or burgers for a week and then drop eggs, cheese, or ham. Eventually, you will not be eating any animals at all! You won't even miss those foods, because you will feel so good.

When you eat this way, your experience will be like mine. You won't feel deprived. You will find your cravings for animal protein slipping away, because the recipes in this book are so yummy and delectable. You will connect to the earth's energy. Eating this way will make you feel so much lighter, with so much energy—and we all love energy! You will want to tell everyone, so they can feel the same way you do. The recipes in *Simple Pleasures* have health benefits, and the best part is that no animals will suffer.

I am now intuitive about what I eat. I listen to my body and have developed a sense of what it needs to function at its best. I have become sensitive to how I react to foods—what makes my eyes puffy, what brings me down, what makes me feel bloated, heavy, and tired, or on the positive side, what gives me energy, makes my skin glow, and keeps me light and happy.

For me, meat substitutes do not work. I don't enjoy food that pretends to be something else. I really don't want to eat bacon, hot dogs, sausage, or meatballs. I would rather eat fresh vegetables, grains, beans, and nuts. For many people who are making the transition to a cruelty-free diet, eating tempeh, seitan, and tofu satisfies the taste for animal products. I have included recipes that use these foods—like shepherd's pie made with seitan, or spinach-tofu lasagna, because so many vegetarians and vegans love cooking with them. If I am feeding serious carnivores, I will sometimes serve tempeh, seitan, or tofu.

I do use some faux ingredients that help me be creative. It's hard to cook certain foods without a substitute for butter—I like Earth Balance—or mayonnaise—Vegenaise is delicious. I like hemp or almond milk, and molasses, cane sugar, agave, and stevia are all great. I use egg replacer for eggs, and there are many different cheese substitutes out there. Try them all and pick your favorite. I happen to like Diaya. Most of these substitutes are delicious, so you won't notice a difference. They are becoming more and more widely available, so check your grocery store. If they don't have these products, ask them to stock them. I have found most stores are happy to do it. I also find great stuff online.

Notes from My Friends

Tanya Petrovna is the co-owner and head chef of four Native Foods restaurants in Southern California and one in Chicago. Without a doubt she makes the most delicious tempeh I've ever eaten. Since tempeh, seitan, and tofu are slowly becoming mainstream, I asked her to talk about them.

Many vegetarians and vegans use these foods regularly as meat substitutes and love them. I do not use these foods a lot, but I have included several recipes in *Simple Pleasures* so you can see how to use them.

**What Is This Stuff Anyway?
A Thumbnail Sketch of
Tempeh, Tofu, and Seitan**

What is tempeh? Tempeh is a whole soy food of Indonesian origin made with a culture. This food is as popular in Indonesia as burgers are in America. I'm seeing tempeh becoming more and more popular in this country… so move aside, burger jive!

I've been making my own fresh tempeh from scratch for twenty-five years. Once you have fresh, you can't go back. Making tempeh is complicated. Whole dried organic soybeans are soaked, hulled, cracked, boiled, and then the water is drained off. The cooked soybeans are mixed with a cooked grain. I love millet. A culture starter is added, as you would add a culture to sourdough bread, yogurt, or miso. The mixture is then spread out about a half inch thick and kept in an eighty-five-degree clean room. The result after about twenty-four hours is remarkable. What were loose grains and beans is now solidly held together by the mushroom-like culture. Slice a piece, sauté it, season it, and watch your inner wow factor rise.

Tempeh is a superfood. Because it's fermented, it strengthens your intestinal flora, and that, my friends, is what builds a strong immune system. Artificial sweeteners along with other chemicals and additives break down your resistance to disease by weakening the effectiveness of intestinal flora. Tempeh can replenish these helpful organisms in your system.

What is tofu? To make tofu, dried soybeans are soaked, finely ground, and boiled. The liquid is put through a sieve, and the ground soybeans are discarded. The fluid that is left is soy milk, thick with the proteins, sugars, and fats from the soybean. A calcium salt is added to the soy milk, which makes it coagulate and form curds. A similar process occurs with cow's milk when cheese is made. The procedure is called separating the "curds from the whey." The soy curds are compressed to produce tofu. It can be marinated, grilled, or baked with spices.

What is seitan? Seitan is still made as it was more than 2,000 years ago in China and the Near East. Wheat flour is kneaded with water and no yeast. The kneading process makes the protein in the wheat flour bind strongly. The dough ball is then submerged in water and kneaded again under the water to remove much of the starch, which is dissolved in the water. What's left is a stretchy-pully-chewy ball of dough that will now get simmered in a full-flavored vegetable broth where it will solidify and expand. The finished product looks like a roast. Seitan is the protein of the wheat. Many versions of seitan can be made to create different textures, and spices can be added for flavor.

Tanya Petrovna
Chef and author of The Native Foods Restaurant Cookbook

Protein Deprivation? No Way!

I am constantly asked, as I'm sure most vegans and vegetarians are, "How do you get enough protein?" Everyone is obsessed with protein. Of course, protein is an important nutrient, but most Americans eat more protein than they need. Dr. Galitzer has given me some facts about this issue.

To start with the basics, proteins are important nutrients that are incorporated into all the vital structures in the body, like bones and muscles. Proteins are also used to create enzymes that initiate chemical reactions. Proteins are composed of building blocks called amino acids. Our bodies are unable to produce nine of the amino acids. Those amino acids are called essential amino acids, not because they are more important to life than the others, but because we obtain these building blocks from the food we eat.

You have probably heard the terms "incomplete" and "complete protein." An incomplete protein does not contain all the essential amino acids; a complete protein does. The fact is that the amino acids in plant proteins are the same as in animal proteins, but not all plant proteins are complete. Vegetarians and vegans do not need to worry about getting a complete protein at each meal. As long as you eat a variety of plant foods from the major vegetarian groups—vegetables, beans, nuts, grains, and seeds—during the course of the day, the body will get all the amino acids it needs to make complete proteins.

The USDA protein requirements are calculated at .36 grams of protein for every pound of body weight, but protein needs vary depending on your age, weight, health, physical activity, body type, and whether you are pregnant or nursing.

Here they are...the faux ones. From the top, clockwise: tofu; tempeh; and seitan.

PROTEIN-RICH VEGETARIAN FOODS

Almond butter • Almonds • Amaranth • Black beans • Black-eyed peas • Broccoli • Brown rice • Bulgur
Cannellini beans • Cashews • Chickpeas • Hazelnuts • Kidney beans • Lentils • Lima beans • Millet
Navy beans • Peas • Pecans • Pinto beans • Potato • Quinoa • Seitan • Soy milk • Soy yogurt • Soybeans
Spinach • Sunflower seeds • Tempeh • Tofu • Veggie burgers • Walnuts • Wheat berries

Grains and legumes—or just plain beans as I call them—are a terrific source of protein. There are special sections with recipes specifically for them. You will find grain recipes in the spring section and beans in the fall section. Also, I've given greens their own section because they are so nutritious. I did this because most people turn up their nose when they hear "greens." Well, no more. The recipes are easy and delicious, so you will never be bored!

Supplements

Vegans and vegetarians do have some special needs when it comes to supplementing their diet. Dr. Galitzer has given me his recommendations for daily supplements for those on a plant-based diet.

Antioxidants

Buffered vitamin C	2,000 mg twice a day
Vitamin E	400 IU daily of a mixed tocopherol product
Quercetin	500 mg daily
N-acetyl cysteine	500 mg daily
Alpha lipoic acid	250 mg twice a day
Zinc	25 mg daily for women; 50 mg daily for men
Selenium	200 micrograms daily

Also essential

Magnesium	250 mg twice daily
Vitamin D	4,000 mg daily
Resveratrol	300 mg daily
Curcumin	500 mg daily

Special needs for vegetarians and vegans as these nutrients are found only in animal products:

Vitamin B_{12}	1,000 micrograms daily
Carnitine	500 mg daily

Fiber, It Is What It Is

One of the most important benefits of eating a plant-based diet is that you will consume lots of fiber. Fiber is a part of the plant that does not break down in your stomach and passes through your body undigested. Consuming 20 to 30 grams of fiber daily can help your body detox. Fiber has been found to reduce the incidence of colon cancer, diabetes, obesity, and heart disease.

There are two kinds of fiber, soluble and insoluble. Soluble fiber holds on to water and forms a gel that slows down your digestion. You feel full longer, because your stomach takes longer to empty out, and that helps with weight control. Blood sugar levels are affected by the delay in digestion, which can help prevent or control diabetes. Soluble fiber can interfere with the absorption of cholesterol from your food and reduce bad LDL cholesterol, a significant advantage.

A friend of mine, a conservative cardiologist, once told me that eating more fiber every day could add ten years to your life. This was a casual conversation, and his statement may have been an exaggeration, but he was very convincing about the importance of fiber.

SOURCES OF SOLUBLE FIBER

Apples • Barley • Berries • Broccoli • Brussels sprouts • Carrots • Celery • Chia • Cucumbers • Flaxseeds Jerusalem artichokes • Legumes (peas, soybeans, lentils, and other beans) • Nuts • Oat bran • Oats • Oranges Pears • Plums • Prunes • Psyllium husks • Rye

Insoluble fiber adds bulk and passes through the intestinal tract mostly intact. It helps to maintain regular bowel movements and keep toxins from building up in your intestines.

SOURCES OF INSOLUBLE FIBER

Avocado • Barley • Bran • Broccoli • Brown rice • Bulgur • Cabbage • Carrot • Cauliflower • Celery Couscous • Cucumbers • Dark leafy vegetables • Flax • Grapes • Green beans • Nuts • Onion • Potato skins • Raisins • Seeds • Tomato • Whole grains • Whole wheat • Zucchini

Notes from My Friends

One day at the gym, I watched a man with the most beautiful physique and posture work out in the most graceful, beautiful way. It turned out he was Jeff DePeron, a personal trainer to the movers and shakers in Los Angeles. He could see that his clients needed to hit the ground running, so he focused on gathering energy from good nutrients. He became a mix master, a juicing genius.

We talked about eating without animals or animal products, and he gave me insights on the nutrients I needed for health and energy. He generously shared two of his brilliant juice recipes, which you'll find on pages 60 and 73.

Don't Lose the Fiber When You Juice

Green foods are most likely the most nutritious foods you can eat. They provide chlorophyll, which rids the body of free radicals that may cause cancer and degenerative diseases. They are also rich in calcium, phytonutrients, sulfur compounds, antioxidants, vitamins, minerals, and amino acids.

Eating raw foods, especially dark leafy greens, gives you energy, ridding the body of toxins that you retain from food, air, water, and stress.

If you make smoothies or juices with a powerful blender, the juice will retain all the fiber in the plant, leveraging all the benefits of the produce without throwing away the fiber, a very

important part of the plant. Fiber serves many important functions, among them stabilizing blood sugar by helping the absorption of sugar into the bloodstream, cleaning out the entire digestive tract, and lowering blood cholesterol levels.

Green juices are loaded with insoluble plant fiber and are also packed with live enzymes that serve as catalysts in every body function. Using a high-power blender to make your juice breaks down walls of cellulose in the plant, predigesting and making the plant's nutrition readily available. Drinking green juices increases your body's ability to absorb nutrients.

JEFF DEPERON
Hura Athletics

Organic Food—Is There Really a Difference?

One of the main reasons I eat organically grown food is simple—it just tastes better. If the flavor isn't enough to convince you that it's worth it, just know that organically produced foods are more nutritious than commercially raised food. They have higher levels of vitamins and minerals, and tons of other benefits.

Organic food is raised under strict government standards. It makes sense to me that eating food that has been produced without antibiotics, hormones, genetically modified seeds, synthetic chemical fertilizer, pesticides, and insecticides has to be healthier. After all, you are what you eat. All those chemicals have a direct effect on your body, and many are toxic.

Notes from My Friends

The Pesticide Load in Food

Pesticides and insecticides encompass a broad range of products that are used inside and outside the home, and in agriculture. They include fungicides that kill mold, herbicides that limit plant growth, disinfectants, and detergents, as well as chemicals that kill bugs and rodents. Pesticides tend to build up in the soil and in streams, rivers, and lakes, eventually finding their way into the food chain. They accumulate on the plants we eat, the grain that is fed to animals that we eat, and in algae, which are consumed by the fish that end up on our plates. Pesticides are fat soluble, which means these toxins remain stored in fat cells throughout the body.

The produce ranked with the highest pesticide load, making them the most important to buy or grow organic, are:

Celery
Blueberries
Cherries
Peaches
Nectarines
Kale and collard greens
Strawberries
Bell peppers
Potatoes
Apples
Spinach
Grapes

The produce listed below has the lowest pesticide load when conventionally grown. They are the safest conventionally grown crops to consume.

Grapefruit
Mangos
Avocados
Sweet peas
Onions
Asparagus
Cantaloupe and honeydew melon
Pineapple
Kiwi
Watermelon

DR. MICHAEL GALITZER

Children are even more vulnerable to these toxins. Think of those little bodies being poisoned while they eat what is supposed to be "healthy" food. There are so many environmental toxins you cannot control, but you can protect yourself and your family by being aware and knowledgeable about what you eat.

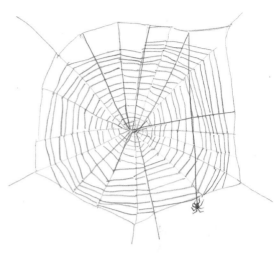

Another plus is that organically raised food is kind to the earth. Organic farming uses half as much energy as commercial farming methods. Organic farming contributes less to global warming, because more carbon locks into the soil, instead of being released into the air. By not using pesticides and other chemicals, organic food production prevents damage to the soil as well as the contamination of streams, rivers, lakes, seas, and oceans. These chemicals harm animals, fish, and insects. They kill off many animals in the wild, disturbing natural ecosystems and reducing their biodiversity, basically destroying Mother Nature.

It's good for you, the animal kingdom, and the harmony of our planet. I know it can be expensive, but eating organic food is well worth it.

You Can Be an Organic Farmer Yourself

f you have a backyard, balcony, windowsill, or even a few free inches on a tabletop, you can plant your own organic garden. Kitchen gardens are easy to plant and take care of. It is so handy to have fresh herbs and lettuces right there when you need them. You can be more ambitious if you have a backyard. A small amount of space will yield leaf lettuces, a couple of tomato plants, and herbs that will grow into bushes. With more space, you can plant zucchini, summer squash, eggplant, and cucumbers. Those vines will produce tons of vegetables. I've seen many balconies in New York City with big pots of tomatoes, peppers, and herbs. There are even easy care planters that you can hang. If you don't have access to outdoor space, you can always have a year-round windowsill herb garden or a good-looking planter in a sunny spot.

Fresh herbs make such a difference when you are cooking—they add flavor and fragrance to whatever you are making. They enhance the taste of vegetables and add interest to salad dressings, dips, and sauces. Here are some of my favorite herbs and what I like to do with them.

Basil Probably my very favorite herb. It works well with most vegetables, but especially tomatoes. It's great in salads, pasta, grilled pizzas, stews, and soups. And don't forget pesto!

Chives I love to snip some chives and toss them in a salad. And what can beat a baked potato with chives? They are good with tomatoes and work well with dips, spreads, and soups. Their pale purple blossoms make a great garnish and taste like a mild onion. Chives can spread in a garden very quickly, and they come up every year.

Cilantro If you like to cook Indian, Mexican, or Asian food, you should grow cilantro. It is good mixed in salsas and salad dressings.

Dill Dill looks like a feathery fern—I love to watch it grow. It has a very fresh, grassy flavor. Dill goes very well with green beans, carrots, potatoes, and tomatoes. I use it all the time in soups, casseroles, and sauces.

Marjoram I mention marjoram because it tastes great in guilt-free veggie burgers. It goes well with spinach, green beans, potatoes, and carrots.

Mint I couldn't live without mint in the summer—it's so cooling. It's great in iced tea and all sorts of drinks. I use it on fruits, peas, carrots, sauces, and in marinades for grilled vegetables.

Oregano A staple of Mediterranean cooking, oregano works well with peppers, tomatoes, eggplant, and beans.

Parsley If you grow only one herb, this should be the one. It's great in salads, dressings, soups, pasta, and on most vegetables.

Rosemary This is a very fragrant, strong herb that I use on roasted potatoes and tomatoes and in soups and long-cooking stews. Mediterranean cooking relies on rosemary.

Sage Sage works well in soups and salads. Its flavor is very woodsy.

Tarragon I use tarragon in vinaigrette dressings and sauces. It has a slight flavor of licorice.

Thyme Another Mediterranean favorite, thyme is good in soups and makes tomatoes, lima beans, and summer squash even more delicious.

You can combine these herbs in endless ways—experiment with them and have fun.

Notes from My Friends

Margot Shaw is the quintessential Southern belle. I met her when we were working out side by side on treadmills at the Lowell Hotel in New York. She introduced herself and asked, "Do you think there is a place for a magazine about flowers?"

I said, "Yes, of course."

She told me that so many people had advised her not to try to produce one.

I said, "Follow your dreams. You'll never know till you try. Go and prove them all wrong!" And, boy, did she!

A year later, she called to ask me to be on the cover of her new magazine, *Flower*. She did a beautiful spread of the gardens at Templeton. And the magazine is a big success!

Seasoning Your Home and Table

If you love to garden and you love to cook, then a kitchen garden is the height of luxury and utility—whether in the ground, a window box, or even terra-cotta containers. The first kitchen garden I ever saw, unlike my little rectangle outside the kitchen door, was an entire acre, a beautiful tapestry of color, shape, and texture. Lettuces, thyme, sage, basil, and rosemary are pretty as you please however you grow them.

You taste your tomato sauce, and it needs a little something, so you scamper out the kitchen door or to the balcony or windowsill to snip off some fresh oregano—easy as pie.

Here in the south, we grow a lot of mint for our iced tea and juleps, but beware, it can take over, so give it plenty of room, or its own pot.

Humble or grand, the kitchen garden seasons your home and table, and often saves you from that last-minute run to the farmers' market or grocer. Using the herbs you grow when you cook is a simple way to add new life to tried-and-true recipes.

MARGOT SHAW
Editor, Flower *magazine*

The Most Forgotten Nutrient

I find it amazing that so many of us do not drink enough water, which is the most important nutrient. We cannot live without oxygen, and we cannot live without water. Two thirds of our body is water. Ninety percent of the brain is composed of water, so imagine what being dehydrated does to us, starting with our control center.

Water is very busy in the body. H_2O helps: regulate body temperature and blood circulation • carry nutrients and oxygen to cells • aid digestion • moisturize the air in the lungs • protect organs • detoxification • move and protect joints • reduce risks of bladder and colon cancer • metabolize fat • rejuvenate skin tissues, moisturize skin, and increase elasticity.

To figure out what your daily intake of water should be, divide your weight by two. That is roughly the number of ounces you should be drinking a day. If you exercise, you will need more. There are free websites that will use a number of factors to calculate how much water you should drink each day. It's worth finding out and sticking to it.

I filter the water I drink and keep a tall glass or bottle with me at all times. Remember: if you wait until you are thirsty, you are too late. If you make a habit of drinking plenty of water, you will not believe how much better you will look and feel.

Notes from My Friends

Joanna Vargas is a skin magician. She knows what works for everyone. Joanna can look at you and know exactly what you need to look and feel better naturally. She also helps her clients with what to eat and juices to drink to maximize the benefits of her innovative treatments. After all, the skin is the largest organ of your body, and it needs proper nourishment as well. The toxins that make you sick affect your skin from the inside out. Using pure organic products and eating plenty of fresh vegetables and fruits will give you glowing, healthy skin.

Why Organic Skincare Products and Cosmetics?

People often ask me, why organic products? In fact, when I opened my salon, many women told me they would be willing to stick with chemicals if that meant they'd get a better result.

I have been an esthetician for fifteen years, and I see the best results with organic and natural products. Studies have shown that chemical-free products penetrate the layers of skin faster without triggering the body's defense mechanisms. Often products that contain chemicals cause inflammation to the skin, which has been proven to be the first detrimental step in the aging process.

Over the course of my career, I have worked with doctors and estheticians alike. I have observed again and again that the body responds best to organic products. If you feed the skin the right mix of vitamins and nutrients, your skin can be better than you ever imagined.

As the beauty industry focuses more and more research on advances in the antiaging industry, I feel that the remedies of the past are more effective than any laboratory creations we've seen thus far. I am more inclined to recommend a yogurt mask from the kitchen than a serum made with special nano-particles. I give my clients recipes for homemade masks and juices so that people can begin to think of the skin as a live organ that needs TLC from the inside out.

When it comes to the body, there are no shortcuts. Good health and looking your best are linked more than you can imagine. I believe that everyone can have beautiful, glowing skin!

JOANNA VARGAS
Joanna Vargas Skincare

Now that you have the basics on the benefits of eating organic food, more vegetables and fruit, and reducing or eliminating animal products in your diet, I hope you are ready to see how eating this way will change your life. If you are "almost" vegan or vegetarian, I hope my recipes will make you want to go a step further. At the very least, you'll be inspired to eat more fruits and veggies. And if you are already vegan or vegetarian, you can try these simple and scrumptious recipes on your friends.

A wooden gate going
into the Topiary Garden.
We try to keep the dogs
out, but it never works!

CHAPTER 3

Effortless Entertaining

The holidays at our house were always happy times, filled with wonderful traditions. Christmas was always black tie, a beautiful dinner with lots of holly and paperwhites everywhere. But my favorite is Thanksgiving. I was born on Thanksgiving Day, so we always celebrated my birthday on Thanksgiving. Wherever we were, we would sit down to eat at one or two. It was always early, so that friends and the people who helped us could go home to celebrate the holiday.

Every year, my mother and I would have the same argument at Thanksgiving. She loved her turkey plates, which I still don't like! This was a battle I let her have, because Christmas came next—and that was the war I really wanted to win. I loved to do Christmas Eve dinner on the later side and use only candlelight—and lots of chocolate for dessert.

Like most children, I loved Christmas Eve. My father wore a red velvet dinner jacket to dinner, and all the dogs wore red bows. The Christmas tree was beautiful, big with lots of lights and bulbs that we've had forever, and I loved all the animals in the crèche. My father always gave me a special present on Christmas Eve.

I've kept up the black-tie tradition. Anyone with no plans, all my orphan friends, spend Christmas Eve at Templeton. Some years it's fifty, some five, and it is always an interesting mix! I love to dress up, but my black-tie dinner is intimate and easy, very different from my parents' parties.

An old sconce—
I love candlelight.

The formal entertaining of my parents' day is outdated, but it is what people often have in mind when they consider having a party or friends over to eat. That image is enough to keep people from entertaining at all—it's so far from the way we live. Everything is so much more relaxed now—from the food to the tables. People appreciate home-cooked food. So many eat on the run, order takeout, or meet friends at restaurants.

Entertaining does not have to be stressful. Simple food served simply is the best. No muss, no fuss is my motto, unless I plan a party with pomp and circumstance. But even then, it doesn't need to be over-the-top. Understatement is key—no one likes pretension.

I love simplicity. I like to take the best of what Mother Nature gives us, keep it as close to its original natural state as possible, and use it to make life more enjoyable. Whether flowers or food, less is best.

Entertaining should be effortless and fun. What's better than a bunch of friends having a lovely dinner? It's work, but when it all comes together—delicious food and wine and lots of laughter—your friends will go home with wonderful memories. To me, that's what it's all about.

So many people tell me they are intimidated by the thought of entertaining. Aside from holidays, the good china and the silver come out once a year. An elaborate menu is planned, usually around an expensive cut of meat, prepared perfectly, and served to impress. The conversation often matches the "best behavior" tone of the party—stiff. Or there's the payback cocktail party when the hosts reciprocate for a year's worth of invitations with cocktails and hors d'oeuvres or maybe even a buffet. I'm not a great fan of cocktail parties. They have no structure. People come and go, catching up with friends or meeting new people superficially. Cocktail parties have their place, but they rarely feel personal. During these parties, I always sense the host is counting the seconds till everyone goes home.

Entertaining is a learned skill. It's like riding or playing the piano. The more you do it, the better you get. I can say that from my own experience. It's more than just kitchen skills, which will also improve the more you use them. It's the whole package—picking how you want to entertain, the guest list, the food, the table. If you do it enough, entertaining becomes a pleasure.

When I came back from California, I entertained a lot. I fed hundreds of people in three years. Entertaining has become second nature to me. Nothing makes me happier than having friends come to the house and cooking delicious food. I find the time I spend planning and cooking dinner—be it for two, twenty, or two hundred—is the best therapy ever.

Though my parents didn't cook, I grew up spending time in the kitchen, where I watched their French chef, Roger, prepare wonderful food. We don't eat the way they did then, when a pound of butter a day kept the doctor away. I grew up loving to cook and bake. It's nurturing, and I find it's a creative outlet that makes me happy. I enjoy it so much that I started my own catering and cookie businesses.

Notes from My Friends

My favorite person in the world to cook with is Michael Guerrieri, a magnificent Italian chef. He can turn vegan ingredients into masterpieces. He has taught me so much in the kitchen. His love of food and respect for ingredients is incomparable. I asked him to give us his thoughts on the subject of sharp knives, which are so important when you are facing a pile of vegetables—especially tomatoes! You will cut your preparation time in half if you know how to handle a knife.

Fearless Knife Handling

The sharpening of knives and what procedures I use to do so depends on how much I care about the knife. For my favorite knives, the ones I have had for years, I wouldn't think of using anything but a stone with a few drops of olive oil. I would use a modern electric sharpener for community kitchen knives at my restaurant. When sharpened this way, the blades get a bit less mileage, but it does the job.

Having a sharp knife is very important when you prepare food, but sharp knives can be intimidating for some. The truth is that a well-sharpened knife can only work its magic when there is a good connection between you and the knife. If too much of your focus goes toward the possibility of cutting yourself, cooking isn't pleasurable. Think of it this way: you are more likely to slice yourself with a dull knife. The math is easy. The extra pressure you need to slice or cut with a dull knife increases the chances of slipping.

Build a good trusting relationship with your knife and master the cutting board. To do that, practice with a large chef knife. Hold the knife upside down, with the cutting edge up. Get comfortable with your stroke and speed by leaning the knife—sharp side up—against your bent knuckles as you practice. Pretend that your fingers are the vegetables you are slicing. You'll be slicing and dicing like a chef in no time.

MICHAEL GUERRIERI
Chef and Owner of
City Sandwich, New York City
and Mezzaluna, Lisbon

You can get over entertaining anxiety. Just accepting that you don't have to be extravagant and pull out all the stops for your friends should help you to relax. I always go for simplicity and fun rather than formality and perfection—from the way the table is set to the menu. You don't want to be stuck in the kitchen or dealing with too many fussy details that can go wrong. If you don't feel up to a dinner, try a weekend brunch or lunch or maybe a Sunday supper. A little thought and effort will make it easy for you to create a casual, comfortable atmosphere that will not only please your friends but will also allow you to enjoy your own party.

Adventures in Cooking

My relaxed attitude comes from surviving hundreds of kitchen disasters. I've learned that if something can go wrong, it will. That's why simplicity and planning are so important. And if things still don't go smoothly, it's all about being able to laugh it off! Even if I make a complete mess of the food, I know my friends and I will stick together through the good and the bad—at least I tried. The bigger the catastrophe, the more I can learn from it. And I can tell you I have had lots of disasters!

Rush at Your Own Risk

One time, I was using a mandoline, a hand-operated slicer that makes thinner slices than a food processor. I was working very quickly, slicing fennel and zucchini, because I was running late. I was making Veggie Carpaccio (recipe on page 126), and I wanted the veggies to marinate in the dressing for a while before I served it. There I was, slicing away at full speed, when next thing I knew, I had sliced the top of my finger. It was hanging by a thread—I stuck it back on. There was blood everywhere. I wrapped the finger as tightly as I could and held my right hand up in the air to stop the bleeding. I wedged the mandoline between some cookbooks and pots and started to work with my left hand.

Luckily, the first guest to arrive was my friend Dr. Brian Saltzman. He walked into the kitchen—we always gather in the kitchen—and saw me with my bloody, wrapped hand over my head, slicing the zucchini furiously.

"What happened to you?" he asked. "Let me see that finger."

The last thing I wanted was for Brian to be stitching me up when my other friends arrived. "I have no time to stop," I explained.

He looked at my finger, stopped the bleeding, and bandaged it. And then he helped me cook! He's great with knives.

Lesson: Beware of the mandoline.

Another lesson: Make sure you leave enough time to prepare the food without having to rush and try to do as much as you can ahead of time. You will be so much more relaxed if you are realistic about how much time it takes to cook the food. That's why you'll find preparation time for each recipe in this book along with the total time. Sometimes an ingredient has to soak for hours. You might have to bring a big pot to a boil, and you know the old saying about a watched pot. Other ingredients might have to cool or marinate before you can continue. Don't get caught running out of time. Being in a frenzy is no fun, and you want to enjoy yourself. If you're stressed, everyone will be stressed... and accidents do happen.

Notes from My Friends

One of Jeff DePeron's great juices will help put you in a frame of mind to work calmly and efficiently in the kitchen. Not only is this juice delicious, but it will also de-stress you as you work.

Jeff's Juice: Bliss Smoothie (Focus and Quiet Energy)

This smoothie promotes feelings of well-being, focus, and quiet energy. The combined ingredients make for a drink that is rich in antioxidants and protein and promotes good digestion, reduces fluid retention, and detoxifies. This recipe makes two servings.

Have a Bliss Smoothie for breakfast or as a snack.

1 cup mixed berries (strawberries, blueberries, blackberries, raspberries)
½ cup mango
2 dates, pitted
½ cup pineapple
Fresh mint
½ inch wedge ginger
14 ounces unsweetened almond milk

Throw all the ingredients in a powerful blender for 2 minutes.

JEFF DEPERON
Hura Athletics

The Art of Camouflage

Another time, I had a major baking disaster. I like to serve fresh baked desserts warm. The house smells so good when people come in if I've just taken a cake, cookies, or pie out of the oven. My friends were on their way as I pulled two cake pans from the oven. The middle of both layers was completely raw. I cut out the center of one layer, cut up the cooked part of the second cake, and filled up the hole in the middle of the first with those pieces. I frosted my one layer, putting berries and chocolate on top. I knew it was a mess, but when I brought it out with a smile on my face, everyone loved it. No one had a clue!

Lesson: Don't panic and be creative if you have a mishap. Many mistakes are salvageable or at least can be covered up.

Another lesson: If you are worried about the food, have a backup on hand. You can keep olives, nuts, and pasta in your house. With fresh vegetables, it's not hard to whip up a salad or pasta dish. As for dessert, always have store-bought ice cream and fresh fruit and lots of dark chocolate on hand!

Final lesson: There is no reason to feel insecure about the food you are serving. If you are, you are probably trying too hard. When you are deciding what you are going to serve, keep it simple and in your comfort zone. That way, you should be able to avoid kitchen disasters.

Natural Disasters and Hidden Resources

We lost our electricity at Templeton on the weekend of a big storm that left two to three feet of snow on the ground. I had some house guests and was expecting six more friends to join us for dinner. We lit candles and lanterns all over the house. No one canceled, because they were all coming in one SUV.

Luckily, my stoves and ovens are gas. I had a frozen piecrust and made a chocolate tart with it. I also had some dried mushrooms, which I soaked, and then I sautéed the reconstituted mushrooms with garlic. I defrosted a container of pesto I had frozen at the end of the summer. With those ingredients, I made a hearty pasta to eat in front of a big fire with some grilled bread, salad, red wine, and a chocolate tart for dessert. It was a perfect dinner for a snowy night.

Lesson: A well-stocked freezer can be a lifesaver. In the fall, try being a smart little squirrel and store things away in your freezer. If you grow your own vegetables, you will always have extra tomatoes, squash, and eggplant. If you don't have your own vegetable garden, you can buy bushels of tomatoes, big bunches of basil, and piles of squash at the farmers' market or your supermarket and get busy.

I make tomato sauce that I freeze for the winter. I slightly sauté eggplant and squash and freeze those. I don't season the vegetables until I use them.

Pesto is one of life's great gifts. It gets me through the winter. It defrosts fast, people love it, and there is no end to what you can do with it. It tastes great on vegetables, pasta, dips, on a sandwich, or as a sauce.

You should have some pesto cubes in your freezer. You never know when you'll need them. I also like to keep frozen piecrusts on hand for a last-minute main-course tart or dessert. Pizza dough is another must-have. With fresh vegetables, you can whip something up in no time. I'll have cookies, a pie, or a tart in the freezer that I've baked as a backup. When I'm baking, I sometimes double the recipes so I'm stocked up.

Notes from My Friends

Chef Michael Guerrieri's pesto sauce is my favorite. I use this recipe all the time. It's the best!

Chef G's Perfect Pesto Sauce
MAKES 1 CUP

1 cup olive oil plus a bit more
  if the puree is too thick
2 garlic cloves
½ cup roasted pignoli
  (pine nuts),
  divided into two parts
1 pound fresh basil leaves,
  all stems removed,
  divided into two parts
  Salt and pepper to taste

Preparation:
1. Pour 1 cup olive oil in the bottom of a blender. Add 1 garlic clove and ¼ cup pine nuts.
2. Fill the blender with the basil, working with only ½ pound, and begin to blend.
3. Turn off the blender from time to time to push down the leaves.
4. Once the mixture begins to rotate on its own in the blender, begin to add the rest of the first ½ pound of the basil.

5. Season with a bit of salt and pepper.
6. You may have to add a bit more olive oil gradually during the puree. The result should be the consistency of soft ice cream.
7. Repeat these steps with the remaining ½ pound of basil and combine in a bowl in the end.
8. Place the pesto in jars, cover with a thin layer of olive oil, and place in the refrigerator or freezer.
9. Most recipes call for Parmesan or Romano cheese. I like to keep the pesto base natural and the cheese optional, which works for vegan cooking. You can add cheeses later when preparing your dishes.

NOTE 1
We often associate the word *pesto* with the traditional "pesto Genovese"—made with basil and cheese. You can easily substitute the basil in this recipe with parsley, spinach, cilantro, mint, or even fresh dill. You can use any of these

pestos for pastas and for seasoning grilled or oven-roasted vegetables and toasts.

NOTE 2
Place the pesto into ice cube trays to make easy-to-work-with pesto cubes. Once they're frozen, pop the cubes out as you would ice and store them in a freezer bag. This makes using pesto a snap.

1. Boil pasta.
2. In the meantime, add some garlic in a frying pan with some olive oil.
3. Once garlic browns, remove pan from heat, add 3 pesto cubes per serving of pasta, and cover while the pasta is cooking.
4. When the pasta is ready, drain and add it to the pesto pan.
5. Mix well and serve.

MICHAEL GUERRIERI
Chef and Owner of
City Sandwich, New York City
and Mezzaluna, Lisbon

When All Else Fails

Afriend invited me for a weekend, and I offered to cook dinner on Saturday night. I loaded a basket from my garden and off I went. Little did I realize their oven was quite different from mine.

I made a veggie tart with zucchini, eggplant, and fennel, put it in the oven, and went to get dressed for dinner. I came back a half hour later to check it, and it was burnt to a crisp—inedible. It was supposed to cook for forty-five to fifty minutes, but the oven was very hot.

Everyone was outside having a drink, waiting for some delicious food. I looked in the refrigerator and the cabinets desperate to find something I could throw together. But there was nothing!

I went outside and told my host that I was on my way into town to get us dinner. I ordered a big bowl of pasta and a salad. Boy, did I wish I had my frozen pesto with me that night! It would have saved the day.

Lesson: You can always order out if the food is a total mess. That is the ultimate backup plan.

These are only a few of the many near catastrophes I have had entertaining. I have learned that I can get through whatever happens, and so can you. Just take a deep breath, relax, smile, and have fun. If nothing else, these disasters make great stories. Once you have survived a few, your confidence will grow, and you'll be able to handle any hurdles the kitchen gods may throw your way.

Sometimes parties are just clunkers. Silence and conflicts are always a bit scary. All you are responsible for doing is putting fun people and good food together in a nice setting. The rest is up to your guests. There are

Notes from My Friends

Most people worry about whether or not their pets will bother people. The fact is that having a party can be disastrous for pets. There are a number of toxins your critters might be exposed to if guests feed them or unknowingly leave something that they can get into. Dr. Palmquist gave me this surprising list of threats for domestic and wild animals. Though it goes beyond party risks, it does cover many threats you should be aware of.

Dr. Palmquist's List of Common Environmental Threats for Animals:

1. Xylitol is a common sugar replacement for diabetic humans, which kills dogs by destroying their livers. A few sticks of gum can be enough to cause major problems for a dog. *http://www.huffingtonpost. com/richard-palmquist-dvm/ common-sweetener-can-kill_b_739534.html*

For a list of common products containing xylitol, see *http://ocd_hs.org/ima_ges/ Xylito_l_Products__2010.doc*

2. Human medications are a common source of poisoning in dogs and cats. Use care in handling your medicines and never give them to your pets without a veterinarian's instruction. *http://www.aspca. org/pet-care/poison-control/ top-10-human-medications-that-poison-our-pets.aspx*

3. Common household plants can be very toxic. Many people don't know that just a few pollen grains from certain lily flowers can cause kidney failure in cats. Here is a great resource: *http:// www.aspca.org/pet-care/ poison-control/17-common-poisonous-plants.aspx*

4. Chocolate, grapes, raisins, bread dough, and onions are just a few foods that can severely affect your pets' health. Chocolate has caffeine-like chemicals that damage the nerves, heart, and brain. Grapes and raisins can lead to kidney failure and death. Consuming as few as eight raisins can be fatal in sensitive pets. The yeasts in bread dough can be problematic for some pets. Onions damage red blood cells and can lead to anemia. Keep food and treats out of your pets' reach and ask guests not to feed your critters.

5. Pets will play and ingest sparkly decorations, so consider whether you really need balloons, ribbons, wrapping paper, or tinsel, and be mindful that they can be dangerous for animals inside your home and out.

6. Be sure pets are properly restrained and protected if you are planning a party with music or sudden loud sounds. Costume parties can alarm pets as well. We need to use caution so they are not injured or frightened into biting or running away.

7. When venturing into the wilderness for hiking and camping, never throw out your chewing gum or the wrappers. Small rodents ingest gum, and it blocks their intestinal tracts, leading to painful death. Always wrap and carry out spent gum as you would any other trash.

8. Reducing your use of plastics may help save species like sea turtles, who accidentally eat plastic thinking it is a tasty jellyfish. The plastic blocks their digestion and leads to disease and death.

Richard Palmquist, DVM
*Chief of Integrative Health,
Centinela Animal Hospital,
Inglewood, California*

times when the chemistry just does not work. People don't click, and the party never takes off. Hey, it happens. When it happens to me, I pick up the pace and end the party as soon as I can. I shrug my shoulders, laugh, and think, Well, that's the way the cookie crumbles. If you have a clunker, at least you get an A for effort. You win some, you lose some!

Notes from My Friends

Michael Guerrieri, my chef friend, eats cruelty-free for long periods of time. I asked him to give me examples of how he constructs a meal without meat that will please every palate.

Your Guests Won't Even Miss the Meat

You are invited for dinner and looking forward to the food that will be served. Your first course is a spinach salad with roasted pignoli and diced dates with a light balsamic lemon dressing. The next course is oven-roasted eggplant stuffed with olives, garlic cloves, diced parsley and topped with seasoned crumbled corn bread to give it a crunchy topping, served over a bed of seasoned tomatoes fresh from the garden. A pear poached in pineapple juice with fresh ginger and a hint of cinnamon with a good cup of coffee finishes the meal. Everyone at the table walks away happy and full. Chances are no one has missed the meat or fish. Satisfied taste buds immediately draw the conversation to how scrumptious the food was.

It's not a difficult task to avoid eating meats when we don't think about it. Instead of slapping a steak on a grill, purchase some extra-large white mushrooms, scoop out the insides with a small spoon and chop the insides with some asparagus, shallots, salt and pepper, breadcrumbs, olive oil, and herbes de Provence. Stuff the mushroom caps with this mixture and place them on the grill or in the oven. Allow them to cook on low heat. The caps will eventually fill with their natural juices to moisten the stuffing. Gently remove them from the heat and serve over your favorite grilled bread slices. A wonderful puree of potato can easily be substituted for the bread. Think about all the earthy, solid foods you can serve to satisfy the palate. No one will ever question a good meal, whether it is composed purely of vegetables or not.

Being a chef, I work with a tremendous variety of foods. Through the years, my body and digestive system always feel and work their best when I treat them to a long term "no meat" routine.

MICHAEL GUERRIERI
Chef and Owner of City Sandwich, New York, and Mezzaluna, Lisbon

Planning a Party Is like Watching a Plant Grow

Planning to have friends and family come over to your house is like watching a plant grow. The whole situation can take on a life of its own. If you set it up right, it grows into something full and rich. You can start with a date, a guest list, and then figure out what to eat, where you will eat, and how to serve it.

I always let my friends know what to expect when I invite them. I'm more comfortable when I know if I'm going to an intimate dinner for six, a pool-side buffet for twenty, cocktails and hors d'oeuvres, a laid-back afternoon in front of the TV on football Sunday, or a seated formal dinner. It sure takes the guessing out of how to dress and helps me get ready for the party.

My decisions about entertaining depend entirely on the season. Clearly, the atmosphere of a party is determined by the weather. A clear spring day, a muggy summer evening, a crisp fall morning, and a stormy winter night call for very different menus and looks. Since I am committed to eating seasonal foods, the first thing I have to consider is what is available. I have included a chart in each seasonal section of this book of vegetables and fruits that are available at that time of year to help you with your planning.

I no longer serve animal products to my friends. At first, I wanted to please everyone, but I felt like a hypocrite cooking with animal products. I wanted to show people how amazing food can be without meat, poultry, fish, butter, and eggs.

One party I'll always remember is the birthday dinner I had for myself a few years ago at my house. It was a black-tie seated dinner with lots of dear friends. They were serious carnivores from Europe, and I planned to serve a cruelty-free dinner. I served quinoa, eggplant and zucchini fritters with a garlic tomato sauce, seitan stew with a red wine base and mushrooms, and roasted root vegetables.

My friend Richard Brown from Amagansett Wine and Spirits sent the most delicious organic wines for dinner. Richard understands how to pair wine with vegan food. In case you are interested, his selections were:

WHITES: Domaine Leflaive Bourgogne Blanc; Huet Vouvray Le Mont Second

REDS: La Spinetta Barbera Ca di Pian; Antoniolo Gattinara Grotto (a Nebbiolo from Piedmont); Collosorbo Brunello di Montalcino Riserva; Alain Graillot Crozes Hermitage

Avoiding animal products does not mean you have to give up wine! But go organic. You'll feel better the next day.

I love dessert and made lots for this event. We had chocolate cake, vanilla cake, apple tart, and my cookies. I didn't tell anyone that the entire meal was vegan until we were finished. I wanted everyone to realize that there are delicious alternatives to a meal full of food that hurts animals. It worked! No one believed it was vegan. They all loved it.

Notes from My Friends

I asked Richard Brown of Amagansett Wine and Spirits for advice on what wines to drink with vegan food. He knows what he is talking about.

Pairing Wine with Meat-Free Food

Vegan cuisine often features a variety of spices in order to achieve flavor and interest. For example, to balance the heat from a spice such as a curry powder, wines modest in alcohol level and perhaps with even a small amount of residual sugar, but not sweet, work best. In whites: Riesling and Gewürztraminer from Alsace or a Chenin Blanc–based wine like Vouvray from the Loire Valley pair nicely. For reds: look for a fruity Gamay wine like a Cru Beaujolais from Burgundy. A well-crafted Cru Beaujolais in a good vintage year is a far cry from, and should not to be confused with, the hyped Beaujolais Nouveau released each November.

Acidity is another characteristic to consider in a dish. If you are using acidic ingredients—tomatoes or citrus ingredients, for instance—you should select wines that are also high in acidity for balance. The acids will neutralize one another, allowing for heightened enjoyment of both the food and wine. In whites, a Sauvignon Blanc or Pinot Grigio is an excellent choice, and for reds, Sangiovese, Grenache, or Zinfandel match well. In Tuscany, Sangiovese is one of the principal grapes grown. Since the native cuisine often includes tomatoes in some form, a Chianti or Brunello di Montalcino from the region is a natural and delicious choice to serve.

Vegetables, both root and green, earthy mushrooms, and herbs typically go well with wines based on grape varieties that share a similar flavor profile. A crisp and herbaceous Sauvignon Blanc from Sancerre or Pouilly-Fumé in the Loire or a steely un-oaked Chardonnay from Chablis in northern Burgundy make for lovely white wine accompaniments to dishes that feature these components prominently. For reds, Pinot Noir from Burgundy, Oregon, or California, a Tempranillo from Rioja, or a Syrah-dominant blend from the Rhône Valley makes for a classic combination.

In warmer months, think about a well-chilled dry rosé that universally complements almost any cuisine. While prepping in the kitchen for one of Cornelia's delectable recipes, nibble on some nuts and sip a glass of dry sparkling wine, prosecco, or Champagne, depending on your level of decadence!

RICHARD BROWN
Amagansett Wine and Spirits

believe that planning a menu is like building a house. You have to use the best materials possible, and for food, that means the freshest. Sometimes I go out with my friends to the berry patch to pick their dessert. You will find such a wide choice of seasonal recipes in *Simple Pleasures*—more than 150—that it will be easy to make delicious food for your friends. Figure out what to serve one course at a time and then start to set your table.

Set a Lively Table

I love to decorate tables. It sets the mood. Sometimes beautiful china, silver, and glasses are the way to go. I like my formal dinners to be elegant but never stuffy. I prefer being casual, and remember...elegance is natural, charming, and fun.

I love to use mismatched plates and glasses. I mix formal and exquisite or fancy with very whimsical things. The contrast is fun and very personal. I collect dishes, serving pieces, bowls, platters, cups, glasses, and vintage table linens. I get them anyplace I can. They always make me smile.

I like to bring nature inside. Luckily there is a ton of stuff to choose from all over Templeton. There are crocus, tulips, hyacinths, and daffodils in the spring as well as apple and peach blossoms, rhododendron, lilacs, and forsythia. The roses and peonies peak in June. We have poppies, hydrangea, allium, snapdragons, honeysuckle, jasmine, lantana, sunflowers, and dahlias—I love the big ones—in the summer. The holly is so beautiful in the winter, and the orchids that have been collected over the years come in from the greenhouse.

I keep centerpieces easy and uncomplicated, not overdone and structured. Don't make anything too tall. There is nothing worse than not being able to see across the table. I use lots of cups and bottles. I especially love old Mateus and tequila bottles. I'll put flowers all over the house, a single flower in unexpected places. A single flower in an old bottle put in between the paws of my ceramic dragon puts a smile on everyone's face. Flowers in powder rooms are a must.

Flowers are so colorful in the spring, but I also use fruit in baskets on the table. I can eat the fruit later or give it away. Nothing ever goes to waste. There are always the donkey, tortoise, other critters, or the compost pile. In the summer, seashells, beach glass and stones, roses, and arrangements of vegetables are great. I love wildflowers and let them grow everywhere. Loose wildflowers in a mason jar are relaxed and summery. I scatter acorns, pinecones, and colored leaves on the table in the fall. In the winter dried hydrangea, berries, witch hazel, evergreens, holly, and orchids work well.

I love to plant bulbs in pots in the winter—paperwhites, hyacinths, tulips, and amaryllis add color and smell wonderful.

Generally, I set the table early in the day for a dinner, a breakfast, brunch, or lunch. It's one less thing to think about. And if you don't like the way it looks, you'll have plenty of time to change it.

Pamper Yourself

If you have planned well, you will have some time to relax before your friends arrive. It beats last-minute stress and conflict. Some of my friends tell me they end up fighting with everyone in the time leading up to a party as they frantically try to pull it all together. Who hasn't had crazy arguments in the kitchen when everyone is waiting? Don't cut it too close. Build in extra time and do as much as you can the day before. Pick recipes that don't keep you in the kitchen all night. Go enjoy yourself and spend time with your friends. Isn't that why you invited them over?

I have pre-party rituals that work for me. I always get some sort of exercise the day of a party to clear my mind and burn off tension, and I like a catnap before dinner. My favorite part is doing one of Joanna Vargas's scrubs and at-home facials. This one is great.

Notes from My Friends

This recipe is great as an exfoliation for the face and body. Joanna tells me that exfoliation is the step no one really takes time out for, and yet it makes the most visible difference to my skin in both summer and winter. This terrific facial is made from ingredients you can find in your kitchen or supermarket.

A Facial from the Kitchen
  ½ fresh coconut, grated
  1 teaspoon turmeric powder
  ¾ pound carrots, grated
2½ cups almond oil
      (or an oil of your choice)
  5 tablespoons rice powder
  1 peeled cucumber, grated

You can combine this mixture by hand or in a blender. Stand in a nice steaming shower and gently rub the mixture over your whole body. The turmeric is an anti-inflammatory ingredient. It also reduces the redness of a sunburn or the swelling of a breakout. The cucumber is depuffing and good for elasticity, while the carrot has great vitamin C. Scrub for five minutes, then rinse.

Joanna suggests following this scrub with a nice hydrating fruit mask.
  2 cups vegan yogurt
  ½ cup warmed vegan honey
  1 handful mashed
      blueberries
  1 handful mashed
      raspberries

Combine all the ingredients and mash together or blend. Apply all over the face and neck.

I like to lie down with two cooled chamomile tea bags on my eyes for depuffing as well. Rest for twenty minutes, then rinse with tepid water. After this scrub and facial, I feel radiant and my skin is soft and supple.
                    JOANNA VARGAS

Notes from My Friends

Instead of having a sip of wine or a drink before guests arrive, try Jeff DePeron's energizing juice, Brazilian Thunder. It will vitalize you without revving you up too much. You will be the perfect, thoughtful, attentive host.

Brazilian Thunder

This kale and açaí drink delivers powerful nutrients that will remove toxins from your body and supercharge you. I often make this juice when I get up in the morning, but wait on days that I am entertaining. The active ingredients of this juice have powerful qualities.

- Kale is rich in chlorophyll, calcium, iron, vitamin A, and fiber.
- Açaí has more antioxidants than blueberries, pomegranate, or red wine and contains essential fatty acids, amino acids, calcium, and fiber.
- Green tea protects against coronary artery disease and cancer, prevents osteoporosis, improves insulin sensitivity in type 2 diabetes, and so much more.
- Coconut water balances the body's electrolytes.
- Mint strengthens heart muscle and contains detoxing compounds.
- Ginger has anti-inflammatory properties and will aid digestion.
- Cinnamon blocks inflammation and bacterial growth.

4 kale leaves
4 ounces unsweetened açaí puree
8 ounces unsweetened green tea
8 ounces coconut water
¼ cup fresh mint
1 inch piece of gingerroot
Dash cinnamon

Throw all ingredients into a high-power blender for 2 minutes.

I love this juice and use it for an energy boost before guests arrive.

JEFF DePERON
Hura Athletics

The Rules of the Game

You have put a lot of thought, planning, energy, and hard work into creating a good time for your friends. I have a few secrets that work for me to make sure things run smoothly. It's all about timing. As the host, make sure nothing drags on. Let people know what time you would like them to come, and if things get late, just sneak off to bed. People will get the message and go home.

My first rule is **never let cocktails go on for too long**. I think a half hour is enough, and sometimes will stretch it to forty-five minutes; if it's a dinner for more than a hundred, maybe an hour.

I don't serve a lot of food before dinner. I like people to be hungry when they sit down to eat. Keep it light—nuts, crudités with hummus, and pea pâté will fill the bill.

If you are having a cocktail party, you need a lot of different food, so no one leaves hungry. How many times have you left a cocktail party starving?

Never wait for people who are late. It's rude to everyone else who got there on time. If you're more than a half hour late from the time you were invited, call to let your host know. I don't wait for anyone. When the food's ready, we eat. I don't wait for anyone when it is time to start.

Don't plate food. I never do. It's old-fashioned. I like people to serve themselves from passed platters or a buffet. That way they can eat what they want, and there is not a lot of wasted food. I hate waste!

If you are seating a party, don't worry about past history. A few times I've had friends tell me they are coming with people who don't get along with others at the party. I don't worry about it. I put people where I want to. I like to mix it up. If it doesn't work, it doesn't work. You never know. Sometimes the best things come out of the worst situations. I once sat two friends who weren't speaking next to each other. After a couple of drinks, they were laughing and were best friends again.

Do not tolerate seat changing. If people change place cards or move, I show them the door! My attitude is, if you are not enjoying yourself here, go someplace else. I have no patience for rudeness.

At one party, I sat next to someone who actually turned his back to me, left the table, and never came back to his seat. I laughed so hard—he really had no manners. My poor host was mortified! My advice is that if you are seated next to someone you find boring, annoying, or offensive, rise to the occasion! Charm the pants off him—that's why you were invited.

I love desserts and serve lots of them. I serve a variety of desserts, especially cookies and dark chocolate. I think it's fun, and they look great after a good meal. If people are on diets, they can just pass.

I hope my advice has put entertaining in perspective and helped to take the terror out of having people over. There is nothing to be worried about. Simple food served casually makes entertaining a joy rather than a trial. What matters is bringing friends together for a relaxed good time.

The easy-to-make recipes in the remaining pages of *Simple Pleasures* will give you ideas for affordable, healthy, delicious food, which will make everyone want more! Once you get the hang of it, you'll never stop!

PART 2

SPRING

I love this old ceramic menu card, it's fun to use
and it's something we no longer see a lot.

Menu

June 7, 2011

Dinner

Tempeh Pot Pie
Vegetable Carpaccio
Grilled Bread
Cucumber Cooler
Domaines Ott Rosé

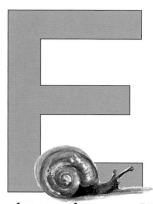arly spring is all mud and rain. Mother Nature is waking up. It is a time of fresh beginnings, of things to come. Nature takes on that early, delicate green. Vegetables push their little noses up through the dirt. Daffodils, tulips, and forsythia color the landscape. The apple trees in my orchard bloom. I open all the windows and doors to let in the fresh air. The birds are busy building their nests. Soon baby animals are everywhere. It's time to plant and prune. WARNING: When pruning, always know where your fingers are! If you don't, you might not like where they end up.

Sweet baby peas, asparagus spears, spinach, and all kinds of lettuces come first. Delicate white flowers that smell so good produce the most delicious strawberries. Rhubarb also comes into season, and with strawberries make a pie that tastes like spring.

Spring flowers are my favorites. The scents of peonies and lilacs let you know that the earth is fully awake and summer is coming. I love peonies everywhere. And in June, the roses begin to blossom. Do your best to get roses that smell, they are much nicer!

I've always had a flower by my bed. My mother said it was good to wake up and go to sleep seeing something beautiful. I keep up the tradition in my room and for all my houseguests.

After winter, nature comes alive with color. I am including a list of spring flowers—trees, shrubs, annuals, and perennials—that you can plant or pick or buy to celebrate spring. I love to bring nature inside with flowers, leaves, branches, you name it. I also love a single, sweet flower in a small bottle. To me, it shows Mother Nature's beauty in the simplest way.

The gate was my grandmother's, Vivian Wessel, my mother's mother. She had it at her house in Boston.

SPRING FLOWERS
Apple blossom • Azalea • Bleeding heart • Brodea • Calla lily • Cherry blossom • Columbine Cornflower • Coral bells • Daffodils • Delphinium Dianthus • Dogwood • Forget-me-not • Forsythia • Freesia Gardenia • Geranium • Heather • Helleborus • Hollyhock Honeysuckle vine • Hyacinth • Iris • Jacob's ladder Laurel • Larkspur • Lilac • Lily of the valley • Lobelia Magnolia • Myrtle • Peach blossom • Peony • Phlox Poppy • Primrose • Pussy willow • Ranunculus Rhododendron • Rose • Statice Stock • Sweet pea • Sweet woodruff Trillium • Tulip • Viburnum Violet • Virginia bluebells • Weigela • Wisteria vine • Zinnia

After a gray world of winter, I love to gather all the forsythia from my garden I can in one armload, bring it into the house, and drop it in a glass cylinder vase. It's a herald of the hope and promise of spring—a burst of sunshine in the living room. Besides, anyone can cut branches, as long as you have a sturdy pair of clippers!

MARGOT SHAW
Editor, Flower *magazine*

Tulips on a
spring table
in an old
polo trophy
my father won.

Nelson guards the Sunchoke Chips.

At the start of spring, Mother Nature gives us a taste of things to come. She has a mind of her own like every female. She loves to tease—a warm summer day, a day of cold rain. You can't count on anything from the garden. You have to work with what nature gives you. I always make sure I have plans A, B, C, and D if I am entertaining in the spring. If I plan a lunch outside, it is sure to storm, thunder, and lightning. I love having people for lunch in the spring. The days are still short, but the light is so bright. Even if it pours, I love to see the new green outside.

A PERFECT SPRING LUNCH

Spring is the start of everything, the beginning of nature's bounty.
I love to put a meal together to celebrate having food from the garden to
cook with again. It's exciting to use what spring has to offer to make
a light and colorful lunch.

MENU

Sparkling Iced Cranberry Green Tea

Michael's Chilled Asparagus Soup

Quinoa Salad with Mint and Parsley
with Lemon Dressing

Strawberry Rhubarb Pie

All-Purpose Piecrust

Sparkling Iced Cranberry Green Tea

SERVES 4

TOTAL TIME: 15 MINUTES

Green tea is an antioxidant and cranberry juice is a cleanser. Combine the two, and you have a delicious, refreshing drink with benefits.

⅓ cup agave

⅓ cup water

4 organic green tea bags

2 cups boiling water

½ cup chilled unsweetened cranberry juice

3 cups chilled seltzer water

1. Combine agave and ⅓ cup water in a saucepan and bring to a boil in a saucepan. Remove from heat and let cool for about 10 minutes.

2. Steep 4 organic green tea bags in 2 cups boiling water for 2 minutes. Remove bags and let tea cool. You can put it in the refrigerator to cool more quickly.

3. Combine cranberry juice, tea, and agave mixture and divide among four ice-filled glasses.

4. Top each glass with chilled seltzer.

Michael's Chilled Asparagus Soup

SERVES 4

TOTAL TIME: 30 MINUTES

I am crazy about my chef friend Michael Guerrieri's chilled asparagus soup and persuaded him to share his recipe.

Olive oil

2 medium-size leeks, cut into 1-inch pieces (including the green tops)

3 bunches asparagus, hard white bottoms cut off and tips reserved

3 potatoes, peeled and cubed

Sea salt and pepper

About 2 tablespoons chopped fresh rosemary

About 10 basil leaves

1. In a medium-size saucepan, add a splash of olive oil and cook the leeks on very low heat until soft, about 5 minutes; do not brown.

2. Add the asparagus stems (not the tips) and potatoes.

3. Cover with water, about 4 fingers above the vegetables. Bring to a boil, then reduce heat and simmer until the potatoes are cooked through, about 10 minutes.

4. Puree the soup in a food processor or hand blender to a silky consistency.

5. Season with salt and pepper.

6. Ladle into soup bowls, sprinkle with a bit of rosemary, add a touch of olive oil, and top each with a raw asparagus tip and basil leaves.

7. Save the remaining delicious asparagus tips for a salad or side dish.

Quinoa Salad with Mint and Parsley with Lemon Dressing

Serves 2

Total time: 30 minutes

This salad is not too heavy and not too light. Mint and parsley are abundant in the spring and transform this dish into a lovely spring green. This basic salad is good with everything.

- 2 cups mint leaves, coarsely chopped
- 2 cups flat-leaf parsley, coarsely chopped
- 1 cup cooked quinoa (from about ¾ cup dry)
- 2 tablespoons extra-virgin olive oil
- 2 tablespoons lemon juice
- 1 teaspoon pepper
- 1 teaspoon fleur de sel

1. Toss together mint, parsley, and quinoa in a bowl.

2. Put oil, lemon juice, pepper, and fleur de sel in a covered jar and shake to mix.

3. Toss dressing with quinoa mixture.

Strawberry Rhubarb Pie

Serves 8

Active time: 45 minutes

Total time: 1 hour and 45 minutes

This pie is beautiful, all reds and raspberry tones. The orange juice brings out the tartness of the rhubarb. If you are in a hurry, you can skip the latticework and do a simple top crust.

- 2 pounds rhubarb, cut into ¾-inch-thick pieces
- 1 pound strawberries, hulled and coarsely chopped
- 1 cup cane sugar
- ¼ cup cornstarch
- ¼ teaspoon finely grated orange peel plus 2 tablespoons orange juice
- ¼ teaspoon sea salt
- 3 tablespoons Earth Balance "butter"

1. Preheat oven to 375°F

2. Make the filling: Mix together rhubarb, strawberries, vegan cane sugar, cornstarch, zest, juice, and salt.

3. Make the crust: See All-Purpose Piecrust recipe on page 86.

4. Roll out 1 ball of piecrust to an ⅛-inch thickness on a lightly floured surface.

5. Fit dough into a 9-inch pie plate.

6. Refrigerate while making top crust.

7. Roll out remaining ball of piecrust dough to an ⅛-inch thickness on a lightly floured surface.

8. Cut into at least fifteen ½-inch wide strips using a fluted pastry cutter.
9. Place rhubarb strawberry mixture in chilled piecrust
10. Scatter pieces of Earth Balance "butter" over filling.
11. Weave lattice over top of pie.
12. Bake for 45 minutes to 1 hour, until crust is golden brown.

All-Purpose Piecrust

MAKES 2 CRUSTS
TOTAL TIME: 35 MINUTES

This is the basic piecrust I use for everything. It is easy and foolproof. You can even make it in a food processor. This crust is so light and flaky you would never know that it's not made with butter.

4½ cups whole wheat pastry flour
1½ teaspoons salt
1¼ cups Earth Balance "butter," chilled and cut into small pieces
  8 to 9 tablespoons cold water

1. In a medium bowl, lightly stir together flour and salt with a fork
2. In a food processor, add cut pieces of Earth Balance "butter" to flour and salt and pulse until the mixture resembles coarse crumbs.
3. Add cold water, a tablespoon at a time, pulsing after each addition until pastry just holds together.
4. Shape pastry into a ball with your hands. If it's a hot day, you may have to refrigerate the dough for 30 minutes or so.
5. For a two crust pie, divide pastry into 2 pieces, one slightly larger, and then gently shape each piece into a ball.
6. On a lightly floured surface, roll the larger ball into an ⅛-inch-thick circle, 2 inches larger all around than the pie plate, with a lightly floured rolling pin. If it is hard to roll out, put the dough between two pieces of plastic wrap and roll over the wrap.
7. Roll half of the circle of dough onto the rolling pin, transfer the flat pastry to one edge of the pie plate, and unroll the rest of the dough onto the plate.
8. Gently press dough into bottom and side of plate.
9. Add pie filling.
10. For top crust, roll out the smaller ball as you did for bottom crust.
11. With a sharp knife, cut a few slashes or a design in the center of the top crust.
12. Roll dough onto rolling pin, center dough over filling and bottom crust, and unroll crust as above.
13. With scissors or a sharp knife, trim the pastry edges, leaving a 1-inch overhang all around the pie plate rim.
14. Fold overhang under; pinch a high edge.
15. Bake as recipe directs.

SPRING VEGETABLES AND FRUIT AT A GLANCE

If you want to eat more fruit and vegetables, you should know what is in season. You will find what is locally available at farmers' markets. Smart supermarkets are now stocking locally grown produce, too.

Fruits and vegetables are in season at different times in different regions. The list that follows will give you an idea of what spring produce is available from all over the country.

SPRING VEGETABLES

Artichokes • Asparagus • Baby lettuces • Belgian endive • Broccoli • Chives • Collard greens • Fava beans Fennel • Fiddleheads • Fresh herbs • Green Onions • Morel mushrooms • Mustard greens • New potatoes Okra • Peas • Radicchio • Ramps • Red radishes • Snow peas • Spinach • Swiss chard • Watercress

SPRING FRUITS

Blackberries • Pineapples • Rhubarb • Strawberries

IN SEASON YEAR-ROUND

This is a go-to list of fruits and vegetables that are always in season.

Apples • Avocados • Bananas • Cabbage • Carrots • Celery • Cherry tomatoes Coconut • Lemons • Mushrooms • Olives • Onions • Parsnips • Potatoes

Strawberry Rhubarb Pie.
Sparkling Iced Cranberry
Green Tea. Tulips in old polo
cups. Red Velvet Cake.

Blueberry Crush

SERVES 8
ACTIVE TIME: 20 MINUTES
TOTAL TIME: 1 HOUR AND 20 MINUTES OR
CHILL OVERNIGHT

I love blueberries. They are the greatest antioxidants around. I make this drink without a sweetener. If it is too intense, add a little agave or sugar to taste.

  2 cups blueberries
  ¾ cup water
  ¼ cup cane sugar or agave
  3 cardamom pods
     Crushed ice
  ½ cup fresh lemon juice
     Additional blueberries (optional)

1. Mash 2 cups blueberries in a large, heavy stainless-steel saucepan with a fork or potato masher.
2. Cook over medium-high heat for 3 minutes or until berries begin to release juice.
3. Remove from heat, cover, and let stand for at least 1 hour or overnight.
4. Strain mixture through a sieve into a bowl, pressing berries with the back of a spoon to remove as much juice as possible; discard solids.
5. Combine ¾ cup water, agave or cane sugar, and cardamom pods in a small saucepan and bring to a boil. Cook 2 minutes, or until cane sugar dissolves.
6. Cool completely; discard cardamom pods.
7. To serve, fill a cocktail shaker halfway with ice and add ¼ cup blueberry liquid, 1½ tablespoons cardamom syrup, and 1 tablespoon lemon juice; shake until chilled.
8. Strain drink into a chilled glass. Garnish with additional blueberries if desired. Repeat procedure with remaining ingredients.

Basic Lemonade

Who doesn't like lemonade? I make lemonade from 1 part fresh-squeezed lemon juice to 4 parts water and 1 teaspoon of agave.

Spiked Lemonade

SERVES 4
TOTAL TIME: 10 MINUTES

Adding wine makes lemonade even more delicious.

  2 cups chilled dry white wine
     (Chardonnay, Pinot Grigio, or Muscadet)
     Chilled lemonade
     Lemon wedges, for garnish

1. Divide wine among four ice-filled wineglasses.
2. Top with chilled lemonade.
3. Garnish each glass with a lemon wedge.

Watercress Spread

SERVES 10 TO 12
TOTAL TIME: 10 MINUTES

*This bitter herb is packed with healing
nutrients. It's especially good for a spring
cleansing. I like it really chunky.*

- 2 cups loosely packed watercress
- 1 cup Earth Balance "butter"
- ½ teaspoon finely grated lemon peel
  Pinch of salt

Place all ingredients in a food processor.
Blend until slightly chunky.

Avocado Chive Dip

SERVES 8
TOTAL TIME: 10 MINUTES

*This intensely green dip is perfect
for spring. It's a great way to eat spring
baby carrots raw.*

- 2 avocados, pitted and cut into chunks
- ¼ cup Vegenaise or nondairy sour cream
- ½ cup snipped fresh chives, plus more for
  garnish
- 2 tablespoons fresh lemon juice
  Sea salt and freshly ground pepper
  Cut-up raw vegetables and whole wheat
  pita chips, for serving

1. In a food processor, combine avocado,
Vegenaise or nondairy sour cream, chives,
and lemon juice. Process until smooth,
1 to 2 minutes.
2. Season with salt and pepper to taste;
process until combined.
3. Garnish with chives and serve with
vegetables and pita chips.

Sunchoke Chips

SERVES 8
ACTIVE TIME: 9 MINUTES
TOTAL TIME: 30 MINUTES

You might not be familiar with Jerusalem artichokes, also known as sunchokes, but they are well worth trying. They are delicious and are becoming more popular every day. This is a basic recipe for a crispy snack. Feel free to use different herbs to give the chips an extra kick.

2 pounds unpeeled Jerusalem artichokes (sunchokes), scrubbed
Canola oil, for frying
About 1 tablespoon sea salt

1. Fill a large bowl with cold water. Slice sunchokes into thin rounds about 1/16 inch thick. A mandoline would be a big help. Drop the slices into a bowl of water as you go to prevent browning. Rinse and drain 3 times. Pat very dry with paper towels.
2. Pour 1/2 inch of oil into a large deep skillet. Heat oil to 375°F.
3. Working in batches, fry sunchoke slices until golden brown. Stir occasionally. Use a skimmer to transfer the slices to paper towels.
4. Dust with sea salt to taste.

Everything Spring Vegetable Salad

SERVES 8
ACTIVE TIME: 30 MINUTES
TOTAL TIME: 40 MINUTES

I love a salad with spring veggies, and this one has them all!

3 tablespoons fresh lemon juice
1/4 cup extra-virgin olive oil
1 tablespoon chopped parsley
Sea salt and freshly ground pepper
6 baby carrots, peeled and quartered lengthwise
6 jumbo or 9 regular asparagus stalks, peeled
1/2 cup sugar snap peas, trimmed
4 cups assorted lettuces
4 radishes, julienned
2 white mushrooms, stemmed and thinly sliced
1 fennel bulb, halved, cored, and thinly sliced
1 cucumber, julienned
1 ripe avocado, cut into 2- by 1/4-inch slices
1 cup pea sprouts or broccoli sprouts
1/2 cup raw cashew halves

1. In a small bowl, whisk the lemon juice with the olive oil and parsley. Season with sea salt and pepper.

Everything Spring Vegetable Salad

2. Bring salted water to a boil in a medium saucepan. Add the carrots and asparagus and cook until the asparagus is bright green and the carrots are just tender, about 2 minutes. Use a slotted spoon to transfer the asparagus and carrots to a platter.

3. Add the sugar snap peas to the saucepan and cook until they turn bright green, about 30 seconds. Transfer to the platter and let cool. Cut the sugar snap peas into julienne strips.

4. Halve the asparagus pieces lengthwise, then halve them crosswise.

5. Put the lettuce, asparagus, carrots, sugar snap peas, radishes, mushrooms, fennel, cucumber, avocado, sprouts, and cashews in a large bowl. Add the vinaigrette and toss well. Serve immediately.

Rainy Day Warm Spring Salad

SERVES 4
ACTIVE TIME: 45 MINUTES
TOTAL TIME: 4 HOURS

This salad works well when Mother Nature throws you a wet, cold day. It warms you up but doesn't stuff you.

1 small red onion, very thinly sliced
¾ cup red wine vinegar
   Sea salt
½ cup water
¾ cup extra-virgin olive oil
1 large carrot, julienned
1 parsnip, julienned
8 sprigs thyme
   Pinch of pepper
1 small butternut squash, peeled, seeded, and cut into ½-inch dice
1 small celery root, peeled and cut into ¼-inch dice
2 heads Bibb lettuce, leaves separated and washed

FOR THE PICKLED ONIONS:
In a medium bowl, combine onion with ½ cup vinegar, 1½ teaspoons salt, and ½ cup water and let stand until the onion is lightly pickled, 3 to 4 hours. Drain.

FOR THE WARM VEGETABLE VINAIGRETTE:
1. In a large skillet, heat 2 tablespoons olive oil. Add carrot, parsnip, 4 sprigs thyme, and a pinch of pepper. Season with salt and cook over high heat, stirring occasionally, until tender, about 3 minutes. Put the vegetables on a plate and discard the thyme.
2. Add 2 tablespoons olive oil to the skillet along with the squash, celery root, remaining 4 thyme sprigs, and a pinch of pepper. Season with salt and cook over high heat, stirring occasionally, until squash and celery root are tender, 5 minutes. Discard thyme sprigs.

3. Return the carrots and parsnips to the skillet. Stir in the remaining ¼ cup vinegar and ½ cup olive oil.
4. Toss the Bibb lettuce with the warm vegetable vinaigrette in a serving bowl and top with the slightly pickled onions.

Soba Salad

SERVES 6
ACTIVE TIME: 15 MINUTES
TOTAL TIME: 50 MINUTES

I love soba noodles. They are a crowd-pleaser. This is a colorful salad that looks beautiful in a serving bowl.

1 package soba noodles
1 cucumber
8 radishes
½ pound sugar snap peas
¼ cup extra-virgin olive oil
1 tablespoon soy sauce
2 tablespoons fresh lemon juice
   Sea salt and freshly ground pepper

1. Cook soba noodles as directed, then place in refrigerator to chill (30 minutes).
2. Thinly slice cucumber and radishes.
3. Put sugar snap peas in boiling water for 2 to 3 minutes, then transfer to a bowl with ice water for 5 minutes, or until cool. Cut into halves.
4. Combine ingredients in a bowl and dress with olive oil, soy sauce, and lemon juice. Season with sea salt and pepper to taste.

Spring Dressings

There are so many delicious, colorful lettuces in the spring for wonderful salads. I love these dressings because they are not overpowering. I like to mix my dressings in a jar with a screw-on top. It's easy to mix up the ingredients well just by shaking. Put some dressing on the bottom of a salad bowl, add the greens, and toss. Add more dressing to taste.

Lemon Dressing

SERVES 8
TOTAL TIME: 5 MINUTES

This is my go-to dressing. I use it as the base of every dressing I make. It has a fresh taste and is cleansing to the body.

- 1 cup lemon juice
- ½ cup olive oil
- 1 tablespoon white wine vinegar

Put all the ingredients in an old jar with a cover and shake. Then add garlic, shallots, or anything else you like—this is a base to go anyway you like.

Basic Vinaigrette

SERVES 8
TOTAL TIME: 3 MINUTES

This vinaigrette is another great base. You can add chopped shallots, garlic, and herbs in any combination. You can whip this up so quickly there is no need to buy prepared dressings. Experiment and have fun with it.

- ¼ cup Dijon mustard
- ½ cup red wine vinegar
- 1½ cups olive oil
  Sea salt and pepper .

In a blender, mix mustard and vinegar until thoroughly combined, then slowly add the olive oil. I like my dressing sharp, so I might use only 1 cup of oil. Season with salt and pepper to taste.

Tomato Vinaigrette

SERVES 4
TOTAL TIME: 6 MINUTES

This dressing spices up any salad and adds texture.

- 1 tomato, grated
- 3 tablespoons olive oil
- 1 tablespoon red wine vinegar
- ½ teaspoon finely chopped fresh oregano
- ½ teaspoon sea salt
- ¼ teaspoon freshly ground pepper

Shake together all ingredients in a glass jar with the lid firmly on.

Poppy Seed Vinaigrette

Serves 4
Total time: 10 minutes

This is a great citrus vinaigrette with the added crunch of poppy seeds.

3 tablespoons fresh lime juice
3 tablespoons fresh orange juice
2 tablespoons grapefruit juice
1 teaspoon Dijon mustard
1 teaspoon Vegenaise
⅓ cup plus 1 tablespoon canola oil
1½ teaspoons poppy seeds
　 Sea salt and freshly ground pepper

In a bowl, whisk the lime, orange, and grapefruit juices with the mustard and Vegenaise. Slowly whisk in the oil until the dressing is creamy. Stir in the poppy seeds, season with sea salt and pepper, and serve.

Spaghetti with Asparagus and Pine Nuts

Serves 8
Total time: 40 minutes

Two of my favorite things in a simple, quick, and delicious recipe—what could be better?

1 pound spaghetti
¼ cup olive oil
¼ cup pine nuts
4 garlic cloves, sliced
2 pounds asparagus, trimmed and cut into 1-inch pieces
1 teaspoon sea salt
¼ teaspoon freshly ground black pepper

1. Cook pasta according to package directions; drain and return to the pot.
2. Heat the oil in a medium-size skillet over medium heat. Add the pine nuts and garlic and cook, stirring frequently until golden brown, 1 to 2 minutes. Add the asparagus and cook, tossing occasionally, until just tender, 2 to 3 minutes.
3. Add the asparagus mixture to the pasta pot along with sea salt and pepper and toss to combine. Serve.

Rigatoni with Asparagus, Artichokes, Lima Beans, and Peas

SERVES 8
ACTIVE TIME: 45 MINUTES
TOTAL TIME: 1 HOUR

I can never get enough artichokes.

  1 lemon
  8 baby artichokes
  1 tablespoon extra-virgin olive oil
  1 small sprig fresh rosemary
     Sea salt and black pepper
  ¾ cup lima beans, fresh or frozen
  8 medium asparagus spears, cut diagonally
     into 2-inch lengths
  1 pound large rigatoni pasta
1½ cups shelled fresh English peas or
     frozen peas, thawed
  ½ cup loosely packed fresh tarragon leaves
  6 tablespoons Earth Balance "butter"
  2 cups packed fresh spinach

1. Preheat oven to 375°F.
2. Finely grate 1 teaspoon lemon peel; set aside.
3. Cut lemon in half. Squeeze 1 lemon half into a bowl of cold water big enough to hold all the artichokes.

4. Trim the tough outer leaves on each artichoke until only pale green leaves remain. Cut ¾ inch from the tops; trim stems.
5. Rub all cut surfaces with remaining lemon half to prevent discoloration. Drop artichokes into lemon water and let soak for 3 minutes. Drain and pat dry.
6. Place artichokes, lemon peel, oil, and rosemary sprig in a 9- by 9- by 2-inch metal baking pan. Sprinkle with sea salt and pepper and toss to coat. Cover baking pan tightly with foil and bake until hearts are easily pierced with a small knife, about 15 minutes. Steam will escape when you remove foil from pan, so be careful.
7. Bring a large saucepan of water to a boil. Add lima beans and asparagus. Cook until asparagus is crisp-tender, about 2 minutes; drain and transfer vegetables to a bowl of ice water to cool. Drain and pat dry. Let stand at room temperature.
8. Cook rigatoni according to package directions.
9. Thoroughly combine artichoke mixture and vegetable mixture with peas, tarragon leaves, Earth Balance "butter," fresh spinach, and rigatoni, and serve right away.

Rigatoni with Asparagus, Artichokes, Lima Beans, and Peas. I have no idea where this glass bowl came from, but it's fun to use it as you can see through it.

Baked Vegetable Risotto

SERVES 8 AS A MAIN COURSE
ACTIVE TIME: 25 MINUTES
TOTAL TIME: 1 HOUR AND 15 MINUTES

Baking the risotto makes this so much easier than making it on the stove. It's the perfect comfort food for spring.

- 2 tablespoons extra-virgin olive oil
- 1 small onion, finely chopped
- 1 cup arborio rice
- 3 garlic cloves, finely chopped
- ½ cup dry white wine
- 3½ cups low-sodium vegetable broth
- ½ teaspoon sea salt
- ¼ teaspoon pepper
- ½ pound fresh asparagus, trimmed, cut into 2-inch pieces, and steamed until crisp-tender (about 7 minutes)
- 1 cup frozen baby peas, cooked according to package directions and drained. Fresh peas can be steamed for 1 or 2 minutes.
- 6 ounces baby carrots, halved lengthwise and steamed until crisp-tender (about 7 minutes)
- 4 scallions (white and green parts), thinly sliced
- ¼ cup chopped fresh flat-leaf parsley

1. Preheat oven to 425°F.

2. In a large, deep-sided, ovenproof skillet with a lid, heat the oil over medium heat. Add the onion and cook, stirring, until softened but not browned, about 2 to 3 minutes.

3. Add the rice and garlic and cook, stirring, 2 minutes.

4. Add the wine and cook, stirring, until almost completely absorbed, about 5 minutes.

5. Add the broth, salt, and pepper; bring to a boil over high heat, 5 minutes. Cover the skillet and transfer to the oven. Bake for 45 to 50 minutes, or until the rice is just tender.

6. Remove risotto from oven and stir in the asparagus, peas, carrots, scallions, and parsley, and serve right away.

Minted Potatoes with Peas

SERVES 8
ACTIVE TIME: 20 MINUTES
TOTAL TIME: 50 MINUTES

This recipe offers a different twist on America's favorite vegetable. I use mint whenever I can. The mint keeps the potatoes light.

1¼ pounds baby red potatoes
½ cup fresh or frozen peas
 2 tablespoons extra-virgin olive oil
⅓ cup chopped mint leaves
¾ teaspoon coarse sea salt
    Freshly ground pepper

1. Cook potatoes in a pot of boiling water until easily pierced with a fork, 11 to 14 minutes, then drain and let cool. Halve potatoes.
2. Simmer peas in a saucepan of water until tender, about 4 minutes for frozen peas. Drain and reserve ¼ cup cooking liquid.
3. Crush peas with 1 tablespoon olive oil and 2 tablespoons reserved cooking liquid until mixture is thick and chunky.
4. Toss potatoes with pea mixture, mint leaves, coarse sea salt, and freshly ground pepper. Drizzle with 1 tablespoon olive oil before serving.

Pea Pesto

SERVES 8 ON PASTA
TOTAL TIME: 30 MINUTES

By now you have used all the frozen basil pesto you made at the end of last summer. This sweet, light pesto is a nice change for spring.

2½ cups fresh or frozen peas
 3 tablespoons olive oil
 1 garlic clove
½ cup spinach leaves
 3 tablespoons pine nuts
½ teaspoon sea salt
    Freshly ground pepper

1. Boil water and cook peas for 3 minutes. Drain well.
2. Heat 1 tablespoon olive oil in a large skillet. Add peas and 1 garlic clove and sauté for 2 minutes.
3. Place peas in a food processor with spinach and pine nuts and pulse until coarse.
4. Add 2 tablespoons olive oil and blend. Season with sea salt and freshly ground pepper.

Asparagus with Mint Butter

SERVES 4
TOTAL TIME: 15 MINUTES

I love asparagus, and the mint in this recipe smells delicious.

  1 cup Earth Balance "butter"
  ½ cup chopped mint
     (save some mint leaves for garnish)
  ½ teaspoon coarse sea salt
  ¼ teaspoon freshly ground pepper
  1 pound asparagus, trimmed

1. Put a pot of salted water on to boil, 15 minutes.
2. Melt Earth Balance "butter" with mint, salt, and pepper in a small saucepan over medium heat until just bubbling around the edges, 4 minutes.
3. Cook asparagus in a pot of boiling salted water until bright green and tender, about 3 minutes. Drain.
4. Drizzle a few tablespoons of mint "butter" over asparagus and toss gently to coat. Garnish with mint leaves.

Radish Roast

SERVES AS MANY AS YOU WANT TO MAKE
TOTAL TIME: 25 MINUTES

I love radishes. Roasting them with salt and lemon gives them a fun twist.

     Radishes, trimmed
     Extra-virgin olive oil
     Sea salt or Himalayan salt
     Freshly ground pepper
     Fresh lemon juice

1. Preheat oven to 450°F.
2. Toss radishes with olive oil. Season with sea salt or Himalayan salt and freshly ground pepper. Roast on a baking sheet, stirring once, until slightly tender and charred, about 15 minutes.
3. Sprinkle with more olive oil and fresh lemon juice to garnish.

Braised Vegetables

SERVES 8
ACTIVE TIME: 15 MINUTES
TOTAL TIME: 45 MINUTES

Braising brings out the flavor of these young vegetables while retaining the nutrients.

  1 tablespoon Earth Balance "butter"
  1 bunch radishes, trimmed and
     quartered lengthwise
  1½ tablespoons extra-virgin olive oil
  1 red onion, halved lengthwise and
     thinly sliced
  3 sprigs thyme
     Sea salt
  2 garlic cloves, very thinly sliced
  1 bunch scallions, trimmed and
     halved lengthwise
  ¼ cup dry white wine

1 pound asparagus, trimmed and cut into 1-inch lengths

1 bunch Swiss chard, leaves torn into bite-size pieces, stems cut into 1-inch lengths

½ pound sugar snap peas, trimmed

1 cup vegetable broth

Freshly ground black pepper

1 cup shelled fresh or frozen peas (about 1 pound in the shell)

1 small head Bibb or Boston lettuce, torn into bite-size pieces

1. Heat Earth Balance "butter" in a large skillet over high heat until sizzling. Add radishes and cook on one side until dappled golden brown, about 5 minutes. Turn radishes and sear for 3 minutes more. Transfer to a bowl.

2. Add oil to pan and stir in onion, thyme, and a pinch of salt. Cook, stirring occasionally, until onion is golden brown, about 10 minutes (reduce heat if it starts to burn).

3. Add garlic and cook 30 seconds. Add scallions, cut-side down, and cook until light golden, about 2 minutes.

4. Pour in wine and boil, stirring for 2 minutes.

5. Toss in asparagus, chard stems, and sugar snap peas; add broth. Cover and simmer for 2 minutes. Season with salt and pepper.

6. Toss in chard leaves, peas, and lettuce; season with more salt and pepper. Cover and cook until wilted, about 3 minutes. Serve right away.

Braised Radicchio with Shallots and Peas

SERVES 6
ACTIVE TIME: 5 MINUTES
TOTAL TIME: 15 MINUTES

This unusual combination makes for a tasty dish that is quick to prepare.

2 tablespoons olive oil

2 tablespoons minced shallot

Sea salt

3 cups fresh or frozen peas (thawed if frozen)

¼ cup radicchio leaves

2 tablespoons vegetable broth, divided

2 tablespoons minced fresh parsley

Freshly ground black pepper

1. Heat the oil in a large skillet over medium heat. Add the shallot and a pinch of salt. Cook 3 to 4 minutes, until softened.

2. Add the peas, radicchio, and 1 tablespoon broth. Cover and cook for 2 minutes.

3. Remove the lid and add the remaining 1 tablespoon broth to deglaze the pan. Add the parsley and season with sea salt and freshly ground pepper to taste.

4. Cook until the broth is evaporated and serve right away.

Red Velvet Cake

SERVES 8
ACTIVE TIME: 20 MINUTES
TOTAL TIME: 1 HOUR

When in doubt, serve red velvet cake. Anytime, anywhere—everyone loves it. I like to under bake my cakes. I take the pans out of the oven five to ten minutes early, because the cake continues to bake while it cools and can lose moisture . No one likes dried-out cake.

Baking is a guessing game. Ovens vary so much that you have to learn by trial and error whether your oven is fast, slow, or right on the mark. I have burned things, and I have served raw or undercooked food. Luckily, no one gets sick if there are no animal products in the dish! I figured it out and so will you. Laugh, because it might take a while.

FOR CAKE BATTER:
3½ cups whole wheat pastry flour
 1 cup cane sugar
 2 teaspoons baking soda
 1 teaspoon sea salt
2½ teaspoons cacao powder
 2 cups hemp milk
⅔ cup canola oil
 3 tablespoons red food coloring
 2 tablespoons distilled white vinegar
 1 tablespoon vanilla extract

FOR BUTTERCREAM FROSTING:
 1 cup Earth Balance "butter," at room temperature
 5 cups confectioners' sugar
 2 tablespoons vanilla extract
4½ tablespoons hemp milk

1. Preheat oven to 350°F. Lightly oil two 8-inch round cake pans.
2. To make the batter: In a large bowl, combine flour, sugar, baking soda, salt, and cacao powder. Create a well in the center, add milk, oil, food coloring, vinegar, and vanilla, and mix until thoroughly combined.
3. Divide cake batter evenly between oiled pans. Place pans in the middle of the oven spaced evenly apart. Bake for 25 to 30 minutes, rotating halfway through. When the cakes pull away from the side of the pans and a toothpick inserted into the center of each comes out clean, they are ready.

4. Let cakes cool for 10 minutes in the pans, then run a knife around the edges to loosen them from the sides. Invert one layer onto a plate and then reinvert onto a cooling rack, rounded-side up. Do the same with the other layer on another part of the rack. Let cool completely.

5. For the frosting, with an electric hand or stand mixer, cream the Earth Balance "butter" until it is smooth and begins to fluff. With the mixer on low speed, add confectioners' sugar and fluff for another few minutes. Add vanilla and hemp milk. Combine well, then beat on high until frosting is light and fluffy, 3 to 4 minutes. Add 1 or 2 tablespoons more milk to achieve the right consistency. Cover the icing with plastic wrap to prevent it from drying out until you're ready to use it. Rewhip before using.

6. To frost cake, place one layer, rounded-side down, on a plate or a cake stand. Using a palette knife or offset spatula, spread some frosting over top of the cake. Carefully set the other layer on top, rounded-side down, and repeat. Cover entire cake with remaining frosting.

Chocolate Coconut Squares

MAKES 16 2-INCH SQUARES
TOTAL TIME: 25–30 MINUTES

These are terrific for everyone. Kids love them, and they are great to bring as presents or to donate to a bake sale.

2½ cups rolled oats
  1 cup almond meal
  1 cup unsweetened shredded coconut
 ⅓ cup cacao powder
 ½ cup extra-virgin coconut oil
  1 cup agave
  1 cup dairy-free chocolate chips

1. Preheat oven to 275°F.
2. Combine oats, almond meal, shredded coconut, and cacao powder in a large bowl. Mix well.
3. Combine coconut oil and agave in a saucepan over medium heat. Stir until mixture is hot, not boiling.
4. Pour syrup over oat mixture and stir until well mixed and cooled slightly. Stir in dairy-free chocolate chips quickly but thoroughly.
5. Press the mixture into an ungreased 8- by 8-inch pan and bake for 20 minutes.
6. Remove from oven and cool completely. Cut into 2-inch squares.

GRAINS

Though there are many recipes in *Simple Pleasures* that use whole grains, I've devoted a special section to grains because they are such an important part of a vegan or vegetarian diet. Whole grains are the seed of a plant, and they contain within them the nutrients and energy to support the growth of a plant. That's why they are so nutritious.

Whole grains are a source of protein. In fact, quinoa contains all the essential amino acids. Grains also contain phytochemicals, antioxidants, B vitamins, vitamin E, magnesium, iron, and fiber. They have been shown to reduce the risk of heart disease, stroke, cancer, diabetes, and obesity. And to top all this, they are delicious and add texture to a dish.

The following cooking chart for the most popular grains works as a quick reference. If you soak grains overnight, you can cut the cooking times below by ten to fifteen minutes. Soaking the grains makes them easier to digest, but it is not necessary. It is a good idea to rinse quinoa well in a fine strainer for one to two minutes before cooking. Its natural coating can taste bitter.

TO COOK ANY GRAIN:

1. Put grains and water into a saucepan.
2. Add sea salt—about ½ teaspoon.
3. Cover pot and bring to a boil over high heat.
4. Reduce the heat to low and steam for the cooking time.
5. Test grains for tenderness.
6. If grains need more time and all the water has been absorbed, add ¼ cup water and cook for 5 to 10 minutes more.

You can be creative with grains and treat many of them like pasta. Just add herbs and veggies of your choice and you have a yummy dish.

1 CUP GRAIN	WATER	COOKING TIME	YIELD
AMARANTH	3 cups	25 minutes	2 cups
BARLEY	3 cups	1½ hours	4 cups
BUCKWHEAT/KASHA	2 cups	20 minutes	2½ cups
BULGUR WHEAT	2 cups	15 minutes	2½ cups
CORNMEAL (POLENTA)	2½ cups	20–25 minutes	2½ cups
COUSCOUS	1 cup	5 minutes	2 cups
FARRO	3 cups	45 minutes	2½ cups
KAMUT	3 cups	1¾ hours	2½ cups
MILLET	3–4 cups	20–25 minutes	3½ cups
OAT GROATS	3 cups	30–40 minutes	2 cups
OATS (STEEL CUT)	2 cups	20 minutes	2½ cups
QUINOA	2 cups	15–20 minutes	2¾ cups
SPELT	3–4 cups	40–50 minutes	2½ cups
WHEAT BERRIES	3 cups	2 hours	2½ cups

Farro and String Beans

SERVES 6

TOTAL TIME: 45 MINUTES

Farro is crunchy and easy to prepare. It's a great substitute for rice and is more nutritious.

1 cup farro

2 cups water

  Salt

6 ounces string beans

1 cup pure olive oil, for frying

4 large shallots, 3 thinly sliced, 1 minced

1 cup spelt or garbanzo bean flour

3 cremini mushrooms, thinly sliced

2 tablespoons sherry vinegar

1 tablespoon balsamic vinegar

1 garlic clove, minced

1 teaspoon thyme leaves

¼ cup plus 2 tablespoons extra-virgin olive oil

3 tablespoons salted toasted hazelnuts, coarsely chopped

  Freshly ground pepper

1. In a medium saucepan, cover the farro with 2 cups water and bring to a boil. Cover pan, remove from the heat, and let stand for 15 minutes.

2. Drain the farro and return it to the pan. Add 2 more cups of water and a pinch of salt and bring to a boil. Cook the farro over high heat until al dente, about 10 minutes; then drain well.

3. Meanwhile, in a saucepan of boiling salted water, cook the string beans until crisp-tender, about 5 minutes; drain. Rinse the beans under cold water and pat dry.

4. Heat olive oil in a medium saucepan. In a small bowl, toss the sliced shallots with the flour, separating them into rings. Transfer the shallots to a strainer and tap off the excess flour.

5. Add the shallots to the hot oil and fry over high heat, stirring, until golden, about 5 minutes.

6. Using a slotted spoon, transfer the fried shallots to paper towels to drain thoroughly; season lightly with salt.

7. Pour off all but 1 tablespoon of the oil from the saucepan. Add mushrooms and cook over high heat, stirring, until browned, about 3 minutes. Transfer to a plate.

8. In a medium-size bowl, whisk the sherry and balsamic vinegars with the minced shallot, garlic, and thyme. Whisk in the olive oil.

9. Add the farro, string beans, hazelnuts, and three-fourths of the fried shallots and toss gently.

10. Season with salt and pepper and transfer to a platter or shallow bowl. Garnish with the remaining fried shallots and serve.

Quinoa Sauté

SERVES 8

TOTAL TIME: 50 MINUTES

Here is another take on quinoa, a very versatile grain. There is so much you can do with quinoa, and every bite is full of great nutrients.

> 3 cups water
> Sea salt
> 1½ cups quinoa, well rinsed
> 1 tablespoon olive oil
> 1 small red onion, chopped
> 1 medium zucchini, chopped
> 2 cups cooked shelled edamame
> 2 cups thawed frozen or fresh corn kernels
> 2 ripe Roma tomatoes, chopped
> Freshly ground black pepper
> 3 tablespoons chopped fresh parsley

1. In a large saucepan, bring the water to a boil over high heat. Salt the water and add the quinoa. Reduce the heat to medium and cook for 20 to 30 minutes. Remove from the heat and set aside.

2. In a large skillet, heat the oil over medium heat. Add the onion, cover, and cook until softened, about 5 minutes.

3. Add the zucchini and cook, uncovered, until softened, about 7 minutes, stirring occasionally. Stir in the edamame, corn, tomatoes, sea salt, and freshly ground black pepper to taste. Cook 5 minutes, stirring occasionally, until heated through.
4. Add the quinoa and parsley, stirring gently to combine. Serve right away.

Curried Quinoa

SERVES 8
ACTIVE TIME: 20 MINUTES
TOTAL TIME: 40 MINUTES

Here is another way to make quinoa delicious. I just love curry.

- 1 cup dry quinoa, rinsed
- 2 cups water
- 1 tablespoon curry powder
- 1 teaspoon cumin
- ½ teaspoon ground red pepper
  Pinch of sea salt
- 2 medium carrots, peeled and shredded (about 1 cup)
- 1 (15-ounce) can chickpeas, rinsed and drained
- 3 green onions, thinly sliced
- 2 Granny Smith apples, halved, cored, and chopped
- ¼ cup toasted pumpkin seeds
- ½ cup finely chopped parsley

FOR THE DRESSING:

- 3 tablespoons extra-virgin olive oil
- 1 tablespoon apple cider vinegar
  Juice of 2 limes
  Sea salt and freshly ground black pepper to taste
- 1½ cups mixed greens per serving of salad (about 12 cups total)

1. In a saucepan, combine quinoa, water, spices, and salt. Bring to a boil, cover, then simmer on low heat for 15 to 20 minutes until quinoa turns transparent and liquid is absorbed. Fluff with a fork, cool, and place in a large bowl.
2. Add carrots, chickpeas, green onions, apples, pumpkin seeds, and parsley.
3. Make the dressing: Whisk together olive oil, apple cider vinegar, lime juice, sea salt, and freshly ground black pepper. Pour over the quinoa mixture and toss.
4. Mix into greens and serve.

Barley, Rice, and Bulgur Salad

SERVES 8
TOTAL TIME: 1 HOUR AND 10 MINUTES

Three grains in one salad plus black beans makes for a very nutritious dish.

- ½ cup pearl barley
- 7 cups water, divided
- ½ cup short-grain brown rice
- ½ cup bulgur

1 tablespoon olive oil

3 ancho chiles, stemmed, seeded, and broken into pieces

1 large onion, chopped

2 garlic cloves, chopped

2 quarts vegetable broth

1½ cups canned diced tomatoes

6 sprigs cilantro, plus ¼ cup chopped cilantro

1 teaspoon ground allspice

Sea salt and freshly ground pepper

½ pound shiitake mushrooms, stems discarded, caps thinly sliced

1 (15-ounce) can black beans, drained and rinsed

1 medium carrot, finely diced

1 medium zucchini, finely diced

½ cup salted roasted pumpkin seeds

1. In a medium saucepan, cover the barley with 4 cups of water and bring to a boil. Cover and simmer over low heat until tender, about 35 minutes; drain. Return the barley to the pan and cover.

2. In another medium saucepan, cover the brown rice with 2 cups of water and bring to a boil. Cover and simmer over low heat until tender, about 35 minutes. Drain the brown rice and add to the barley.

3. In a medium bowl, cover the bulgur with 1 cup of hot water. Cover and let stand until the water is absorbed, 10 minutes.

4. In a large, heavy pot, heat the olive oil. Add the chiles, onion, and garlic and cook over moderately high heat, stirring occasionally, until the onion is lightly browned, about 5 minutes.

5. Add the broth, tomatoes, cilantro sprigs, and allspice and season with 1 tablespoon salt and a pinch of freshly ground pepper. Bring to a boil, then cover and simmer over low heat for 45 minutes. Let cool slightly. Puree the contents of the pot in a blender and return to the pan.

6. Add the mushrooms, black beans, carrot, zucchini, and parsnip to the puree and bring to a boil. Cover and simmer over low heat for 20 minutes. Add the barley, rice, and bulgur and season with salt and pepper.

7. Serve in a tureen and sprinkle pumpkin seeds on top; serve extra pumpkin seeds on the side.

Barley and Roast Squash

SERVES 8

TOTAL TIME: 1 HOUR AND 10 MINUTES

Squash is an easy comfort food, one of my favorites.

4 cups butternut squash, peeled and cut into 1-inch cubes

7 small peeled shallots, 1 minced

6 small sage leaves

2 tablespoons extra-virgin olive oil

Sea salt and freshly ground black pepper

3 tablespoons Earth Balance "butter"

2 cups pearl barley

8 cups vegetable stock

¼ cup whole roasted peeled chestnuts, coarsely chopped

2 tablespoons chopped parsley

1. Preheat oven to 375°F. On a large rimmed baking sheet, toss the diced squash with the whole shallots, sage, and 1 tablespoon of the oil and season with sea salt and freshly ground black pepper. Roast for 40 minutes, turning once, until the squash and shallots are softened and browned in spots. Crumble the sage. Leave the oven on.
2. In a large enameled cast-iron casserole, melt 1 tablespoon Earth Balance "butter" in the remaining 1 tablespoon oil. Add the barley and cook over moderate heat, stirring, until golden, 7 minutes. Add the minced shallot and cook until softened. Add the vegetable stock and bring to a boil, 30 minutes. Season with sea salt and freshly ground black pepper. Cover and bake for 35 minutes, or until barley is al dente.
3. Stir the chestnuts into the barley and simmer over moderate heat until the liquid is thickened and nearly absorbed, about 5 minutes. Stir in the remaining 2 tablespoons Earth Balance "butter", the roasted squash, shallots, sage, and parsley. Season with sea salt and freshly ground pepper and serve.

Bulgur Roast Vegetables

SERVES 4
ACTIVE TIME: 5 MINUTES
TOTAL TIME: 30 MINUTES

This hearty grain dish will fill you up.

2 cups coarse bulgur, rinsed

2 cups hot water

1 medium zucchini, cut into ¼-inch dice

1 medium carrot, cut into ¼-inch dice

1 small red onion, cut into ¼-inch dice

¼ cup extra-virgin olive oil

Sea salt and freshly ground black pepper

1 tablespoon tomato paste

¼ cup fresh lemon juice

½ medium cucumber, peeled, seeded, and cut into ¼-inch dice

Red pepper flakes

1. Preheat oven to 400°F. In a large bowl, cover the bulgur with the hot water. Cover the bowl with a plate and let stand until the water has been absorbed and the bulgur is tender, about 20 minutes.
2. On a large rimmed baking sheet, drizzle the zucchini, carrot, and onion with 2 tablespoons olive oil. Season with sea salt and freshly ground black pepper and toss well. Roast for about 15 minutes, until the vegetables are slightly softened. Remove from oven and let cool on the baking sheet.

3. Fluff the bulgur with a fork. Stir in the tomato paste. Fold in the roasted vegetables, lemon juice, cucumber, and remaining 2 tablespoons olive oil. Season with sea salt, freshly ground black pepper, and red pepper flakes.

4. Serve at room temperature or slightly chilled.

Roast Vegetable Polenta

SERVES 6

TOTAL TIME: 1 HOUR AND 25 MINUTES

Creamy, yummy, warms your tummy.

3¾ cups vegetable broth

  1 cup polenta

3½ tablespoons extra-virgin olive oil

  4 large garlic cloves, finely chopped

  4 teaspoons chopped fresh lemon thyme

½ teaspoon sea salt, plus additional to taste

¼ teaspoon freshly ground black pepper, plus additional to taste

¼ cup balsamic vinegar

¼ cup oil-packed sun-dried tomatoes, drained and very finely chopped or pureed

  5 Italian or Japanese eggplants, cut into 1-inch cubes

  2 medium zucchini, cut into 1-inch-thick slices

  2 medium red onions, cut into eighths

  8 small red potatoes, quartered

1. Preheat the oven to 400°F. Lightly oil a 9- by 5-inch loaf pan and set aside.

2. In a large stockpot, bring 3½ cups broth to a boil over high heat. Slowly add the polenta, stirring constantly with a long-handled wooden spoon. Reduce the heat to low and stir in 1 tablespoon oil, half the garlic, half the thyme, sea salt, and freshly ground black pepper.

3. Cover and cook, stirring occasionally, until polenta is tender, about 15 minutes. Remove from heat and let stand, covered, 5 minutes.

4. Spread the polenta mixture in the bottom of the oiled loaf pan. Let stand until firm, about 20 minutes.

5. Unmold onto an ungreased baking sheet and cut into 12 slices.

6. Brush the tops evenly with ½ table-spoon oil and set aside. In a large bowl, combine the remaining broth and oil, the vinegar, sun-dried tomatoes, and the remaining garlic and thyme. Add the eggplant, zucchini, onions, and potatoes. Season with sea salt and freshly ground black pepper and toss well to combine.

7. Let marinate for about 15 minutes at room temperature. Transfer the vegetables to a large rimmed baking sheet. Bake 30 minutes, or until tender and lightly browned, stirring and turning halfway through cooking time.

Remove from oven and cover with foil to keep warm.

8. Set the oven to broil and broil the polenta slices 6 to 8 inches from the heat source until lightly browned.

9. Place 2 polenta slices on each of six serving plates and top each slice with the vegetables and cooking juices. Serve right away.

Beet and Wheat Berry Salad with Pumpkin Seeds

Serves 4
Active time: 30 minutes
Total time: 2 hours and 30 minutes

I love beets. They contain so much iron. The crunchy pumpkin seeds will add texture to your salad.

- 4 medium beets
- 3 tablespoons extra-virgin olive oil, divided
- 1 cup uncooked wheat berries
- 2 cups water
- ½ cup unsalted pumpkin seeds, toasted and divided
- 1 tablespoon Dijon mustard
- 1 tablespoon sherry vinegar
- ¼ teaspoon sea salt
- ¼ teaspoon freshly ground black pepper
- ⅓ cup diced celery
- ¼ cup thinly sliced shallots
- 2 tablespoons chopped fresh chives

1. Preheat oven to 400°F.

2. Leave root and 1 inch of stem on beets and scrub beets with a brush. Place beets in center of a 16- by 12-inch sheet of foil; drizzle with 1 tablespoon olive oil. Fold foil over beets; tightly seal edges.

3. Bake for 1 hour and 20 minutes, or until tender.

4. While the beets cook, combine wheat berries and 2 cups of water in a medium saucepan and bring to a boil. Cover, reduce heat, and simmer for 1 hour, or until tender, stirring occasionally. Drain; cool slightly.

5. Unwrap beets and let cool. Trim off beet roots; rub off skins. Cut beets into wedges.

6. Place ¼ cup pumpkin seed kernels in a large bowl and coarsely crush with the back of a spoon. Add mustard, vinegar, salt, and pepper and stir well with a whisk. Gradually add remaining 2 tablespoons olive oil, stirring constantly with a whisk.

7. Add beets, wheat berries, and chives to dressing and toss gently. Sprinkle with the remaining ¼ cup pumpkin seeds and serve.

Beet and Wheat Berry Salad with Pumpkin Seeds.

PART 3

SUMMER

Pan holding the iced tea and Winston guarding them!

can finally be barefoot! I love to feel the earth under my feet, especially the mud! I kick off my shoes in the summer and walk barefoot on the warm ground.

Hummingbirds love the feeders that I fill with nectar. The days are so long. I get up early before it gets hot and go out to the garden to decide what to make for lunch and dinner. I don't pick anything until the last minute so that the food is really, really fresh. There is nothing like biting into a tomato right off the vine or a strawberry still warm from the sun!

Hydrangeas mean summer to me—snowball flowers bring summer inside and dry so beautifully. They are a good reminder of summer on cold, dark winter days. Beds of daylilies that close up every night, butterfly bushes filled with butterflies, cleome, or spider flowers, climbing roses and pink and white cosmos make me smile!

Summer's a vibrant time, and there are so many beautiful flowers that bloom through the season. Don't let your plants get too thirsty as the temperature rises.

Tomato Tarte Tatin,
with a beautiful dahlia
I had just picked from
the garden.

SUMMER FLOWERS Allium • Astilbe • Baby's breath • Bachelor's button • Bee balm • Bell flower Black-eyed Susan • Butterfly flower • Calla lily Campanula • Carnation • Coleus • Coneflower • Coral bells • Coreopsis • Cosmos • Dahlia • Daisy • Daylily Delphinium • Dianthus • Foxglove • Freesia • Gardenia Geranium • Gladiolus • Guara • Hibiscus • Hollyhock Honeysuckle • Hosta • Hydrangea • Iris • Impatiens Lady's mantle • Larkspur • Lavender • Lilac • Lilies Lupine • Marigold • Morning glory • Nasturtium • Pansy Petunia • Phlox • Poppies • Ranunculus • Rose mallow Russian sage • Salvia • Sedum • Smoke shrub • Stock Spider flower • Sunflower • Sweet pea • Trumpet vine Verbena • Veronica • Yarrow • Yucca • Zinnia

Trumpet flower.

When I pick blackberries and raspberries, I pop as many in my mouth as I do in the bowl. Every summer I try to figure out ways to get to them before the birds and critters—they always win!

Outside I always use plastic plates, glasses, and tableware and serve iced tea with lots of fresh mint; everything grilled—zucchini, corn on the cob, squash blossoms—tons of pesto, celery with shaved artichokes with lemon and olive oil dressing, ice cream and sorbet with no sugar. Everything very simple.

We toast with rosés, pink champagne, crisp white and chilled red wine. After the salad course, I take everyone to the berry patch where they can pick their own dessert. It's fun, different, and everyone loves it. Summer is a time for wonderful, fresh food and relaxed good times.

I love the sounds and smells of summer nights. Fireflies, croaking frogs, cicadas singing, and clear starry skies. And who doesn't love the smell and sound of the ocean? It makes me sleep so well.

Cooking in the summer is so much fun. I go out to the garden early in the morning to see what's there and plan my menu. I'm always amazed at how quickly everything grows. One day it's a seedling and the next it's an entire

Hydrangeas are summer. From the garden into every room, in every vessel of every sort, hydrangeas are the answer. The temperature drops a good 10 degrees every time you glimpse a cluster of the cool blue or pink or even white blooms. I'm refreshed just thinking about them.

There's no need to "arrange" hydrangeas. They're so full and frothy, they pretty much arrange themselves. Just be sure to remove foliage from below the water line to avoid bacteria in the water.

MARGOT SHAW
Editor, Flower *magazine*

plant with something delicious to eat! I think the energy Mother Nature puts into growing all her wonderful things is so pure that when you eat them you feel better, happier, and you increase your own energy.

There is such an abundance of fresh food in the summer that I like to invite friends for a sampler of dishes with as many ingredients as I can get out of the garden, served buffet-style by the pool. That way there is something for everyone, and I can have fun with the ingredients. I eat often by the pool in the summer—a big buffet with as many ingredients as I can get out of the garden. It's fun to see my friends taste new things and understand how well they can eat just from plants. It's truly a joy to watch people learn and understand that the alternatives to animals are just as delicious and filling. I think even more so!

AN ALFRESCO
SUMMER DINNER

MENU

Iced Tea

Pea Pâté

Grilled Bread

Green Gazpacho

Veggie Carpaccio

Spaghetti with Fresh Tomatoes and Basil

Zucchini Blossoms Stuffed with Amaranth

Green Salad with Truffle Vinaigrette

Plum Pie

Popsicles

Iced Tea

SERVES 8

PREP TIME: 50 MINUTES

Templeton is famous for its iced tea. People constantly ask me for the recipe. Fresh orange juice is the secret ingredient.

2 quarts boiling water
8 herbal lemon tea bags
1½ cups fresh squeezed orange juice
   Fresh mint

Pour 2 quarts boiling water over tea bags. Brew for 30 minutes and let cool. Remove tea bags. Add orange juice and serve over ice with fresh mint.

Pea Pâté

SERVES 6

TOTAL TIME: 30 MINUTES

Sweet spring peas have the perfect flavor and color for this light pâté. You can whip this together in less than a half hour. In other seasons, you can substitute frozen peas, edamame, or lima beans, but fresh peas are the best.

3 cups fresh peas (or frozen peas, edamame, or lima beans)
2 cups sliced carrots
1½ cups fresh cauliflower
2 tablespoons chopped parsley

1 tablespoon pine nuts
   Salt and pepper

1. Steam the fresh peas for 2 minutes (frozen peas, edamame, or lima beans for 7 minutes).
2. Steam the sliced carrots for 7 to 10 minutes depending on size.
3. Steam the cauliflower for 10 minutes.
4. Put all the ingredients in a blender or food processor and blend. I like this pâté chunky.
5. Add salt and pepper to taste.
6. Serve at room temperature with grilled bread, vegetable crudités, pita chips, or on a bed of lettuce. You can make this a day ahead if you refrigerate it covered.

Grilled Bread

TOTAL TIME: 5 MINUTES

Can't live without it. Add herbs and garlic if you want to dress it up.

   Crusty bread or pita bread
   Olive oil
   Sea salt

Slice your favorite pita or crusty bread. Drizzle olive oil on both sides and grill well. Salt to taste.

Green Gazpacho

Serves 2
Total time: 10 minutes

Since I am allergic to bell peppers, I am always finding ways to make gazpacho without them. This a great recipe, and so refreshing on a hot day.

2½ cups shelled fresh English peas
2¼ cups ice water
1½ cups chopped peeled cucumber
 1 cup (½-inch) bread cubes
3½ tablespoons olive oil
1½ tablespoons sherry vinegar
 2 garlic cloves
 ½ teaspoon sea salt
 ½ teaspoon freshly ground black pepper
 1 tablespoon fresh mint

1. Cook peas in boiling water for 4 minutes. Drain and rinse with cold water until cool. Set aside ½ cup peas.
2. Combine remaining peas, 2¼ cups ice water, cucumber, bread, 2 tablespoons olive oil, vinegar, and garlic cloves in a blender. Process until smooth.
3. Stir in sea salt and freshly ground black pepper.
4. Put in a serving bowl and top with reserved peas, mint, and a drizzle of olive oil.

Veggie Carpaccio

Serves 8
Active time: 10 minutes
Total time: As long as you want to marinate the vegetables

Beware the mandoline and your fingertips! Slicers are dangerous. You can serve this freshly made or make it a day or two in advance to allow it to marinate.

 3 fennel bulbs
 3 summer green zucchini
 1 cup chopped shallots
 ½ cup chopped dill
    Olive oil
    Sea salt and pepper
 1 lemon

1. Thinly slice the fennel and zucchini (if you have a mandoline or food slicer, great; if not, get them as thin as possible).
2. In a dish, put a layer of fennel, then zucchini, then sprinkle shallots and dill, drizzle olive oil, and add sea salt and pepper. Continue layering until all your veggies are done.
3. Garnish the top with dill, scallions, a big drizzle of olive oil, and the juice of 1 lemon.
4. Let sit for as long as possible. Can be made one day in advance.

Veggie Carpaccio. Quick and easy to make and so healthy!

Spaghetti with Fresh Tomatoes and Basil

<small>SERVES 8</small>

<small>ACTIVE TIME: 15 MINUTES</small>

<small>TOTAL TIME: 45 MINUTES</small>

This recipe is as basic as it gets. The fresh cherry tomatoes make it special. Boiling the water is the hard part!

Sea salt

½ cup olive oil, plus extra for the pot

6 garlic cloves, minced

4 pints small cherry tomatoes or grape tomatoes

18 large basil leaves, julienned, plus a few extra leaves for serving

2 tablespoons chopped fresh parsley

2 teaspoons chopped fresh thyme leaves

1 teaspoon freshly ground black pepper

½ teaspoon red pepper flakes

¾ pound dried spaghetti

Spaghetti with Fresh Tomatoes and Basil. The perfect summer food! I love linens. I inherited some but am constantly looking for more at swap meets and thrift stores. Friends also bring them to me.

1. Bring a large pot of water to a boil and add 2 tablespoons sea salt and a splash of oil to the pot.

2. Heat ½ cup olive oil in a large sauté pan. Add the garlic to the oil and cook over medium heat for 30 seconds.

3. Add the tomatoes, basil, parsley, thyme, 2 teaspoons salt, pepper, and red pepper flakes. Reduce the heat to medium-low and cook for 5 to 7 minutes, tossing occasionally, until the tomatoes begin to soften but do not break up.

4. While the tomatoes are cooking, add the spaghetti to the pot of boiling water and cook according to package directions. Drain the pasta, reserving some of the pasta water. Place the spaghetti in a serving bowl, add the tomatoes, and toss well. Add some of the pasta water if the pasta seems too dry.

5. Serve in a large bowl with extra basil on the side.

Zucchini Blossoms Stuffed with Amaranth. I use all my green dishes in the summer.

Zucchini Blossoms Stuffed with Amaranth

SERVES 4

TOTAL TIME: 45 MINUTES

Zucchini blossoms are so beautiful. This is so easy to make, and your friends will be very impressed. You can make the stuffing the day before so you can enjoy your friends, stuff the blossoms, and have a great lunch. Amaranth is a gooey grain that works well as a stuffing. I serve this dish with iced tea with mint or a crisp white wine. Fresh tomatoes go well with the squash blossoms.

3 cups amaranth

1 medium onion

3 tablespoons olive oil, divided

2 zucchini

1 small eggplant (you want to end up with 1½ cups after it is cooked)

1 garlic clove

4 large blossoms per serving

1 tablespoon finely chopped parsley

1. Bring 3 cups of water to a boil and add amaranth. Simmer and cook until water is absorbed, approximately 20 to 25 minutes.
2. Quarter the onion and cook in 1 tablespoon olive oil for 30 minutes over medium heat until caramelized.
3. Dice zucchini and sauté in 1 tablespoon olive oil until soft, approximately 5 to 7 minutes.
4. Dice eggplant and garlic and sauté in 1 tablespoon olive oil for 10 minutes.
5. Mix the cooked vegetables with the amaranth and add parsley. Fill the squash blossoms with the mixture. Serve at room temperature.

Green Salad with Truffle Vinaigrette

SERVES 8
TOTAL TIME: 10 MINUTES

I like to mix a variety of salad greens, preferably picked at the last minute. The truffle oil adds depth and an earthy aroma.

Lettuce

FOR THE DRESSING:
- ½ cup lemon juice
- ½ cup olive oil
- ¼ cup truffle oil
- 1 tablespoon white wine vinegar
  Sea salt and pepper to taste

1. Mix dressing ingredients together in a covered jar.
2. Wash and crisp lettuce of your choice. I use Bibb, red leaf, and anything else I can get from the garden or a farmers' market.
3. Put truffle vinaigrette in the bottom of a big bowl, add your favorite lettuces, and, toss well.

Plum Pie

SERVES 8
ACTIVE TIME: 40 MINUTES
TOTAL TIME: 1 HOUR AND 40 MINUTES

It's fun to cook with fresh plums because they are so colorful. This uncommon pie is easy to make and is always a big hit.

- 1 pound pitted, coarsely chopped plums
- ¼ cup cornstarch or whole wheat flour
- 2 tablespoons vegan cane sugar
- 2 All-Purpose Piecrusts (see recipe on page 86)

1. Preheat oven to 350°F.
2. Mix plums, cornstarch or flour, and sugar in a large bowl.
3. Line one pie dish with your piecrust.
4. Pour plum mixture into pie.
5. Cover plums with the other piecrust, cut a hole in the middle or prick with a fork and fasten the sides of the crust together.
6. Bake for 1 hour, or until golden brown.

Popsicles

Popsicles are a great way to cool down. These two recipes are delicious and sweetened with agave rather than sugar, a great alternative that everyone loves.

Watermelon Popsicles

SERVES 8

ACTIVE TIME: 5 MINUTES

TOTAL TIME: 3 HOURS

1½ pounds seedless watermelon without the rind, cut into 1-inch dice (about 4 cups)

2 tablespoons agave

¼ cup mint leaves, minced

Pinch of sea salt

1. In a blender, puree the watermelon with the agave until smooth. Stir in the mint and salt.

2. Pour the puree into eight Popsicle molds or two standard ice cube trays (insert popsicle sticks halfway through freezing) and freeze until hard, about 3 hours.

Pineapple Popsicles

SERVES 8

ACTIVE TIME: 20 MINUTES

TOTAL TIME: 4 HOURS AND 30 MINUTES

¾ cup agave

1 cup water

4 cups finely diced fresh pineapple, divided

1 tablespoon fresh lime juice

1. Bring agave and 1 cup water to a boil in a small saucepan over high heat, stirring for about 30 seconds. Chill syrup until cold, about 1 hour.

2. Puree agave and 2 cups pineapple in a food processor until smooth.

3. Set a fine-mesh strainer over a medium pitcher; strain pineapple mixture, pressing on solids to extract puree.

4. Stir in lime juice and remaining 2 cups pineapple.

5. Divide among molds. Cover and insert Popsicle sticks.

6. Freeze until firm, about 3 hours.

7. Dip bottoms of molds into hot water for 20 to 30 seconds to loosen pops. Remove pops and serve.

Summer Fruits and Vegetables at a Glance

This handy list will remind you what vegetables and fruits are at their peak in summer.

SUMMER VEGETABLES

Arugula • Carrots • Corn • Cucumber • Endive Eggplant • Fennel • Fingerling potatoes • Garlic scapes Green beans • Lettuce • Lima beans • Okra • Peppers Sugar snap peas • Summer squash • Tomatoes • Yukon Gold potatoes • Zucchini

SUMMER FRUITS

Apricots • Blueberries • Cantaloupe • Cherries • Figs • Honeydew melon • Mangoes • Nectarines • Plums • Raspberries • Watermelon

The four summer drink recipes that follow are not only refreshing and cooling, but they also add color to any table.

Strawberry Lemonade

Serves 8
Active time: 15 minutes
Total time: 1 hour

 2 cups water
½ cup agave (more to taste)
 1 cup fresh lemon juice (from 6 lemons), plus 1 lemon, sliced for serving
 1 pound cleaned strawberries
16 ounces seltzer, chilled
   Mint sprigs for serving

1. In a medium saucepan, bring 2 cups water and agave to boil over medium-high heat. Reduce to a simmer and cook, stirring occasionally, until combined, about 1 minute.
2. Transfer to a pitcher and refrigerate until cool, about 45 minutes.
3. Add lemon juice to pitcher and stir to combine.
4. In a blender, puree strawberries until smooth.
5. Pour through a fine-mesh sieve into pitcher with lemon syrup, pressing on solids. Stir well to combine.
6. To serve, stir in seltzer and divide among ice-filled glasses. Top with lemon slices and mint sprigs.

Watermelon Lemon-Lime Cooler

Serves 8
Active time: 20–25 minutes
Total time: 40–45 minutes

1¼ cups water
 ½ cup agave
 ⅓ cup coarsely chopped fresh mint
 1 tablespoon grated lime peel
 1 tablespoon grated lemon peel
12 cups seeded watermelon, cut into 1-inch cubes
 ¼ cup fresh lime juice
 1 tablespoon fresh lemon juice

1. Combine 1¼ cups water and agave in a small saucepan; bring to a boil over medium-high heat. Cook for 30 seconds, stirring frequently.
2. Remove from heat; stir in mint, lime peel, and lemon peel. Let stand 20 minutes.
3. Strain mixture through a fine-mesh sieve over a bowl, discarding solids.
4. Place one third each of agave mixture and watermelon in a blender; process until smooth. Pour puree into a large pitcher.
5. Repeat the procedure twice with remaining syrup and watermelon. Stir in lime juice and lemon juice.
6. Serve over ice or refrigerate until ready to serve. Stir before serving.

Cucumber Cooler

SERVES 8
ACTIVE TIME: 15 MINUTES
TOTAL TIME: 24 HOURS

3 cucumbers, peeled, seeded, and coarsely chopped, plus thinly sliced cucumber for serving
¼ cup water
½ cup fresh mint leaves
1 lime, thinly sliced
1 tablespoon agave syrup
24 ounces club soda

1. In a blender, puree chopped cucumbers and ¼ cup water.
2. Pour through a fine-mesh sieve over a large bowl, pressing on solids. You can prepare 2 cups of juice the day before and chill in the refrigerator.
3. In a pitcher, mash mint leaves with the back of a wooden spoon until bruised, add agave syrup, cucumber juice, thinly sliced lime, and club soda. Stir to combine.
4. Serve over ice with a nearly transparent cucumber slice as a garnish

Southsides

SERVES 1

This tart, sweet, and minty drink delivers a real kick in the pants. If you prepare the simple syrup in advance, this drink takes no time at all. You might want to make a pitcherful on a hot night.

2 sprigs mint
1 lime, cut into pieces
¾ ounce fresh lime juice
1 ounce simple syrup (recipe follows)
2 ounces gin
3-4 ounces soda water

1. Muddle 1 sprig of mint with the lime pieces, lime juice, and simple syrup in the bottom of a bar glass.
2. Transfer to a cocktail shaker. Add gin and shake well.
3. Pour into a glass over crushed ice and stir until the outside of the glass frosts.
4. Top with soda water, garnish with remaining sprig of mint, and serve.

Simple Syrup

MAKES 8 SERVINGS
ACTIVE TIME: 1 MINUTE
TOTAL TIME: 11 MINUTES

Simple syrup is 1 part sugar to 1 part water. It is used in iced tea in the South and in other drinks everywhere.

½ cup unrefined sugar
½ cup water

In a medium saucepan, combine sugar and water and bring to a boil, stirring, until sugar has dissolved. Allow to cool.

Summer Salsas, Spreads, and Dips

Summer is all about easy, basic casual entertaining. You will find that these recipes for healthy, easy-to-prepare snacks and appetizers work well in the heat—not that they sit around for long.

Tomato Corn Salsa

MAKES 1½ CUPS
TOTAL TIME: 5 MINUTES

This dip is great with everything from burgers to wraps. It will be one of your favorites. It's always on my table.

1   cup fresh corn kernels
    (from 2 ears of corn)
1   medium tomato, diced
1   scallion, thinly sliced crosswise
2   tablespoons chopped fresh cilantro
1   tablespoon fresh lime juice
    Sea salt and freshly ground pepper to taste

In a large bowl, combine all ingredients. Toss and season with sea salt and pepper.

Green Tomato Salsa

MAKES 1½ TO 2 CUPS
ACTIVE TIME: 14 MINUTES
TOTAL TIME: 20 MINUTES

Now you know what to do with excess tomatoes.

1   medium Vidalia onion, sliced
2   tablespoons olive oil,
    plus more for brushing
    Sea salt and freshly ground black pepper
1   pound green unripe tomatoes
2   tablespoons chopped cilantro
1   large red tomato, cored and coarsely chopped
1   tablespoon fresh lime juice

1. Light a grill.
2. Brush the sliced onion with oil; season with sea salt and freshly ground black pepper. Grill the onion and whole green tomatoes over high heat, turning once, until charred; about 6 minutes for the onion, 8 for the tomato.
3. Chop the onion into 1-inch pieces and transfer to a bowl. Core, peel, and coarsely chop the green tomatoes and add to the bowl. Stir in the cilantro, red tomato, lime juice, and 2 tablespoons oil. Season with sea salt and freshly ground black pepper to taste.

Lemon Chickpea Puree

MAKES 2 CUPS
ACTIVE TIME: 5 MINUTES
TOTAL TIME: 1 HOUR AND 5 MINUTES

On a cracker or anything toasty,
this spread delivers great protein.

2   cups dried chickpeas, soaked in
     cold water overnight and drained
1   small carrot
1   celery rib
1   small onion, halved
1   small fennel bulb, halved
5   garlic cloves
3   sprigs thyme
1   bay leaf
½ cup extra-virgin olive oil
     Sea salt and freshly ground pepper
½ cup chopped flat-leaf parsley
1   preserved lemon, pulp discarded
     and peel finely chopped
2   tablespoons fresh lemon juice

1. In a saucepan, cover the chickpeas
with water.
2. Add the carrot, celery, onion, fennel,
garlic, thyme, bay leaf, and ¼ cup olive oil.
Bring to a simmer, cover, and cook over
low heat until the chickpeas are tender,
about 1 hour.
3. Let the chickpeas cool in the liquid to
room temperature, then drain, reserving
¾ cup of the cooking liquid. Discard
the vegetables and herbs.
4. Blend chickpeas with reserved cooking
liquid, add the rest of the olive oil, and
blend well.
5. Stir in parsley, preserved lemon, and
lemon juice. Top with a drizzle of olive oil
to serve.

Roast Cauliflower Puree

MAKES 1½ CUPS
ACTIVE TIME: 10 MINUTES
TOTAL TIME: 50 MINUTES

I love the way cauliflower looks as it
grows—its beautiful white face wrapped
in big green leaves. This dish is cauliflower
at its creamy best.

1   head cauliflower (about 2 pounds),
      halved crosswise and thinly sliced
¼   cup olive oil
1½ tablespoons grated fresh ginger
1½ teaspoons ground coriander
      Sea salt
3   tablespoons tahini paste
3   tablespoons fresh lemon juice
3   tablespoons chopped cilantro
      Sesame seeds
      Grilled pita or vegetable crudités
      for serving

1. Preheat the over to 450°F.

2. In a large bowl, toss the cauliflower with the oil, ginger, and coriander and season with sea salt.

3. Spread the cauliflower on a rimmed baking sheet and roast for about 40 minutes, stirring once or twice, until tender and lightly browned in spots.

4. Remove from oven and let cool slightly.

5. Transfer the cauliflower to a food processor. Add the tahini and lemon juice and pulse to a chunky puree; season with sea salt.

6. Add the cilantro and pulse until just incorporated.

7. Transfer the spread to a bowl and sprinkle with sesame seeds. Serve warm with grilled pita or vegetable crudités.

SUMMER SOUPS

I love to serve cold soups in the summer. They are refreshing and very tasty.

White Gazpacho

SERVES 4
ACTIVE TIME: 18 MINUTES
TOTAL TIME: 48 MINUTES

This combination of cauliflower and pine nuts is a fresh take on a classic.

½   medium head cauliflower, cut into 1-inch florets

1½ cups cold water

2   slices whole wheat bread, crusts removed

¼   cup pine nuts

2   garlic cloves, coarsely chopped

1   tablespoon sherry vinegar

1   large shallot, coarsely chopped

1¼ cups blanched slivered almonds

½   medium seedless cucumber, peeled and coarsely chopped, plus ¼ cup finely diced cucumber

⅓   cup olive oil
    Sea salt

1. Preheat the oven to 350°F.

2. In a large saucepan of boiling salted water, cook the cauliflower until tender, about 8 minutes. Strain, rinse under cold water until cool, and let drain well.

3. In a blender, combine 1½ cups cold water with the cooked cauliflower, bread, pine nuts, garlic, sherry vinegar, shallot, 1 cup slivered almonds, and the coarsely chopped cucumber; blend until smooth.

4. Add the olive oil and pulse until just incorporated.

5. If necessary, add more water to thin the gazpacho.

6. Season the soup with salt and refrigerate until chilled, about 1 hour.

7. Spread the remaining almonds in a pie plate and toast for about 6 minutes in the preheated oven, until fragrant and lightly golden.

8. Ladle the gazpacho into bowls. Garnish the soup with the toasted almonds and the finely diced cucumber and serve.

Dill Leek Soup

Serves 4

Active time: 30 minutes

Total time: 4 hours and 30 minutes

Even the colors of fresh dill with leek are cooling. This is a sophisticated soup that will be the main attraction of a light summer menu.

2	tablespoons olive oil
6½	cups (about 5 large) thinly sliced leeks (white and pale green parts only)
1	large russet potato, peeled and cut into ½-inch cubes
4	cups vegetable broth
3	tablespoons coarsely chopped fresh dill, divided, plus dill sprigs for serving
¼	teaspoon freshly grated nutmeg
	Sea salt and freshly ground pepper
1	tablespoon lemon peel, very thinly sliced (yellow part only)

1. Heat olive oil in a large heavy pot over medium heat. Add leeks and cook until softened and wilted, stirring often, 5 to 6 minutes (do not brown).

2. Add potato and stir to coat.

3. Add broth, increase heat to high, and bring to a boil.

4. Reduce heat to medium and simmer until vegetables are very tender, about 15 minutes.

5. Working in batches, puree soup with nutmeg in a blender until very smooth. Transfer to a large bowl.

6. Season with sea salt and freshly ground pepper to taste. Stir in remaining tablespoon dill.

7. Cover and chill for 4 hours. Sprinkle chopped dill and lemon peel.

*Dill Leek Soup.
I found these old
soup bowls at a
swap meet.*

Summertime Soup

SERVES 8
ACTIVE TIME: 30 MINUTES
TOTAL TIME: 1 HOUR

This recipe for a light vegetable soup is perfect for summer.

- 1 tablespoon plus 2 teaspoons olive oil
- 2 medium leeks (white and light green parts only), halved lengthwise, cut into ¼-inch slices, rinsed well, and drained)
  Sea salt and freshly ground black pepper
- 1½ pounds russet potatoes, peeled and cut into ½-inch cubes
- ½ pound string beans, cut into 2-inch pieces
- 4 cups parsley leaves (1 bunch)
- 5 cups vegetable broth

1. In a medium pot, heat 2 teaspoons oil over medium-high heat.
2. Add leeks and season with sea salt and freshly ground black pepper.
3. Cook, stirring frequently, until leeks are soft and lightly browned, about 6 minutes.
4. Add potatoes and string beans and cook for 10 minutes.
5. Add broth, cook for 15 to 20 minutes until the vegetables are tender.
6. In a food processor, combine parsley leaves and 1 tablespoon oil and process until finely chopped. Remove soup from heat and stir in parsley puree.
7. Serve cold or at room temperature.

Cold Tomato and Basil Soup

SERVES 4
ACTIVE TIME: 25 MINUTES
TOTAL TIME: 4 HOURS

This classic is one of my all-time favorites.

- 2½ pounds ripe tomatoes, peeled, seeded, and chopped
- 4 cups vegetable broth
- ¼ cup finely chopped fresh basil plus whole basil leaves for garnish
- 2 garlic cloves, finely chopped
- ½ teaspoon salt
  Freshly ground black pepper to taste
- 2 tablespoons extra-virgin olive oil
- 1 tablespoon red wine vinegar
- ½ tablespoon balsamic vinegar

1. Puree the tomatoes in a blender or food processor fitted with the knife blade.
2. Transfer to a large saucepan and add the broth, chopped basil, garlic, salt, and pepper; bring to a brisk simmer over medium-high heat.
3. Reduce the heat to low and simmer gently 20 minutes, stirring occasionally.
4. Remove from heat and stir in the oil and vinegars. Let cool to room temperature. Cover and refrigerate a minimum of 4 hours, or up to 2 days.
5. Serve chilled and garnish with whole basil leaves.

Summer Salads

Summer is the season for salads. With so much available in your garden and the farmers' market, the combinations are endless. I could do an entire book on summer salads!

Grilled Vegetable Salad

<small>SERVES 8</small>
<small>TOTAL TIME: 25 MINUTES</small>

I love this kitchen sink salad. Just throw it on the grill and mix it up. It's filling and tastes like summer.

- 1 small fennel bulb, sliced lengthwise ⅓ inch thick
- 1 Asian eggplant, sliced lengthwise ½ inch thick
- 1 ear of corn, shucked
- 1 small onion, sliced ⅓ inch thick and separated into rings
- 1 medium zucchini or yellow squash, sliced lengthwise ½ inch thick
- 2 tablespoons extra-virgin olive oil, plus more for brushing
  Sea salt and freshly ground black pepper
- 1½ cups halved cherry tomatoes
- 1 avocado, chopped
- ⅓ cup fresh lime juice
- ¼ cup chopped cilantro
  Grilled bread, for serving

1. Light a grill, brush the fennel, eggplant, corn, onion, and zucchini with oil and season with salt and pepper. Grill over moderately high heat for about 15 minutes, turning often, until the vegetables are lightly charred and tender.

2. Using a large knife, cut the charred corn kernels from the cob and place them in a large bowl.

3. Coarsely chop the remaining vegetables and add them to the bowl along with the cherry tomatoes.

4. Add the olive oil, lime juice, and cilantro to a blender and puree until smooth.

5. Add avocado to the vegetables and toss the salad with dressing.

6. Serve with grilled bread.

Asparagus Slaw

<small>SERVES 6</small>
<small>ACTIVE TIME: 25 MINUTES</small>
<small>TOTAL TIME: 55 MINUTES</small>

A delicious twist on a standard.

- 3 carrots, grated
- 1½ pounds asparagus, grated
- ⅓ cup chopped fresh mint
- ⅓ cup sliced red onion
- 2 tablespoons olive oil
- 1 tablespoon lemon juice
- 1 teaspoon coarse sea salt

Combine all ingredients and serve.

Asparagus Slaw in an old ceramic dish I got from my mother.

Beet Slaw

SERVES 6

TOTAL TIME: 30 MINUTES

What is a picnic or a barbecue without coleslaw? This beet slaw will add color to your table. Love 'em or hate 'em, beets are good for you. You can make this dish the day before.

¼ cup olive oil

2 tablespoons red wine vinegar

¾ teaspoon coarse sea salt

¼ teaspoon freshly ground black pepper

1½ pounds golden beets, peeled and cut into matchsticks

3 scallions, sliced

½ cup fresh chopped cilantro

1. Whisk together oil, vinegar, salt, and pepper.

2. Toss with beets, scallions, and cilantro, and serve.

Watercress, String Bean, and Fried Shallot Salad

SERVES 8

ACTIVE TIME: 30 MINUTES

TOTAL TIME: 45 MINUTES

Fried shallots—need I say more?

1 pound string beans, trimmed

1 cup safflower oil

3 shallots, thinly sliced crosswise into rings

2 teaspoons all-purpose flour

Coarse sea salt

2 tablespoons fresh lemon juice

2 tablespoons Dijon mustard

3 tablespoons extra-virgin olive oil

Freshly ground black pepper

1 bunch watercress, tough stems removed

1. Bring a large pot of salted water to a boil.

2. Prepare a large bowl of ice water and place a colander inside the bowl.

3. Line a baking sheet with a double layer of paper towels.

4. Cook the green beans in the boiling water until bright green and crisp-tender, 2 to 3 minutes.

5. With a wire skimmer or slotted spoon, transfer beans to the colander. Cool green beans completely in ice bath to stop cooking, then transfer to the lined baking sheet; pat dry with more paper towels.

6. In a small saucepan, heat safflower oil over medium-low heat.

7. In a small bowl toss shallots with flour.

8. Working in 3 batches, fry shallots in oil until golden and crispy, 2 to 4 minutes.

9. Transfer shallots to paper towels and season generously with salt.

10. In a small bowl, whisk lemon juice, mustard, and olive oil to combine; season dressing with salt and pepper.

11. Place watercress on a serving platter

and drizzle with half the dressing.

12. Top with green beans and remaining dressing. Serve sprinkled with fried shallots.

Farro and Tomato Salad

SERVES 8

ACTIVE TIME: 1 HOUR AND 10 MINUTES

TOTAL TIME: 9 HOURS AND 10 MINUTES (OVERNIGHT SOAK)

Here is another way to use tomatoes without pasta. Warning: the farro needs to soak overnight.

1	cup farro, soaked overnight and drained and rinsed thoroughly
	Coarse sea salt
6	to 7 cups water
4	tablespoons extra-virgin olive oil
2	tablespoons red wine vinegar
	Freshly ground black pepper to taste
½	small red onion, chopped
4	medium tomatoes, seeded and chopped
1	medium cucumber, peeled, seeded, and chopped
½	cup chopped fresh basil leaves
2	tablespoons chopped fresh parsley or mint leaves

1. Soak the farro overnight.

2. Drain and rinse the farro thoroughly.

3. In a medium stockpot, bring 6 cups salted water and the farro to a boil over high heat.

4. Reduce the heat to between medium and medium-low and simmer, uncovered, until the farro is tender, stirring occasionally, about 40 minutes, adding water if necessary to prevent the farro from drying out.

5. Drain the farro in a colander and rinse with cold water.

6. In a large bowl, whisk together the oil, vinegar, sea salt, and pepper.

7. Toss farro with vegetables, herbs, and dressing and serve right away.

Radicchio, Arugula, and Fennel Salad

SERVES 6

TOTAL TIME: 20 MINUTES

I love fennel, which adds extra crunch and flavor to this salad.

3	tablespoons pine nuts
¼	cup fresh orange juice
3	tablespoons extra-virgin olive oil
1½	tablespoons red wine vinegar
	Sea salt and freshly ground pepper to taste
1	medium fennel bulb, trimmed, quartered, cored, and thinly sliced
1	medium head radicchio, cored and torn into bite-size pieces
1	(10-ounce) bag arugula

1. Heat a small heavy-bottomed skillet over medium heat. Add the pine nuts and toast, stirring constantly, until light brown and

fragrant, about 3 minutes. Immediately remove the nuts from the skillet and set aside.
2. In a large bowl, whisk together the orange juice, oil, vinegar, salt, and pepper until thoroughly blended. Stir and add the fennel, radicchio, and arugula; toss well to combine. Let stand for about 10 minutes. Serve with reserved pine nuts.

Grilled Corn and Avocado Salad

SERVES 6
TOTAL TIME: 25 MINUTES

There is nothing like sweet summer corn. This pairing is smooth and crunchy, colorful, and totally delicious.

 4 ears of corn, shucked
 1 avocado, sliced
 ¼ cup chopped fresh cilantro
 1 tablespoon fresh lime juice
 1 tablespoon extra-virgin olive oil
 ½ teaspoon coarse sea salt

1. Heat a grill to medium-high. Grill corn, rotating often, until lightly charred, about 15 minutes.
2. Let cool slightly. Carefully cut kernels from cobs.
3. Gently toss corn kernels with avocado, cilantro, lime juice, olive oil, and salt. Serve right away.

Grilled-Bread Panzanella

SERVES 6
ACTIVE TIME: 30 MINUTES
TOTAL TIME: 45 MINUTES

I like to use a variety of tomatoes in this classic dish. They add great color and different flavors.

 6 ounces string beans, trimmed
 2 to 3 thick pieces crusty bread
 ¼ cup olive oil plus more for brushing
 1 pint cherry tomatoes, halved, or 2 large tomatoes, coarsely chopped
 5 large basil leaves, torn
 ½ red onion, thinly sliced
 ¼ cup red wine vinegar
   Sea salt and freshly ground black pepper

1. Blanch string beans in a large saucepan of boiling water until just tender, about 5 minutes. Drain and let cool.
2. Brush bread lightly with olive oil. Grill the pieces directly on a medium grill, turning until just starting to char, about 3 minutes.
3. Cut grilled bread into 1-inch cubes
4. In a serving bowl toss bread cubes with beans, tomatoes, basil, and red onion.
5. Whisk together vinegar and oil and season with salt and pepper. Pour over salad and let stand for 15 minutes. Season with salt and pepper and toss so that the bread absorbs any remaining dressing. Serve right away.

*Grilled-Bread Panzanella.
This one gets you in and
out of the kitchen fast on
a hot summer day.*

Pappardelle with Parsley-Mint Pesto

SERVES 8 (MAKES 2 CUPS PESTO)
ACTIVE TIME: 30 MINUTES
TOTAL TIME: 45 MINUTES

This pesto is a good use for all that mint in your garden. Make sure to use wide pasta so that the pesto sticks to it. You can freeze the pesto for a taste of summer all year-round.

1 cup packed flat-leaf parsley leaves
1 cup packed mint leaves, plus mint sprigs for garnish
3 garlic cloves, coarsely chopped
¼ cup walnuts
½ cup extra-virgin olive oil
   Sea salt and freshly ground black pepper
2 medium zucchini
1 pound dried pappardelle

1. In a food processor, combine the parsley, mint, garlic, and walnuts and pulse until coarsely chopped.
2. Pour in the olive oil and process to a puree. Season the pesto generously with salt and pepper.
3. Cut each zucchini lengthwise into paper-thin strips with a mandoline or vegetable peeler, using the outsides of the zucchini only. Discard the seedy centers.
4. In a large pot of boiling salted water, cook the pappardelle until al dente.
5. Add the zucchini to the pot, stir once, and drain, reserving ¼ cup of the pasta cooking water.
6. Return the pappardelle and zucchini to the pot. Add the pesto and the reserved pasta water and toss. Season with salt and pepper.
7. Transfer the pasta to a large bowl and garnish with mint sprigs.

Grilled Polenta and Radicchio

SERVES 8
ACTIVE TIME: 1 HOUR
TOTAL TIME: 3 HOURS

This is a great dish for entertaining. You can make the polenta the day before and finish it on the grill.

2 cups water
2 cups hemp milk
2 garlic cloves, smashed
1 sprig rosemary
1 sprig thyme
1 cup instant polenta
   Sea salt and freshly ground black pepper
1 cup balsamic vinegar
2 medium heads of radicchio, cut into 1-inch-thick wedges through the cores
   Extra-virgin olive oil, for drizzling and brushing

1. Lightly oil a 9-inch square glass or ceramic baking dish.
2. In a medium saucepan, combine the water, hemp milk, garlic, rosemary, and thyme, and bring to a boil.
3. Remove from heat and let steep for 10 minutes.
4. Discard the garlic, rosemary, and thyme, and return the mixture to a boil.
5. Gradually whisk in the polenta and simmer over low heat, whisking often, until very thick and no longer gritty, 10 minutes. Season with salt and pepper.
6. Pour the polenta into the baking dish. Let cool to room temperature, then cover and refrigerate for at least 2 hours.
7. In a small saucepan, boil the balsamic vinegar over moderately high heat until reduced to ¼ cup, about 15 minutes. Let cool to room temperature.
8. Light a grill. Drizzle the radicchio wedges with olive oil and season with salt and pepper. Grill over moderately high heat until lightly charred and just tender, about 3 minutes per side.
9. Carefully unmold the polenta and cut it into 8 wedges or squares.
10. Brush all over with olive oil. Grill the polenta until it's lightly charred on the bottom, about 4 minutes per side.
11. Arrange the grilled polenta and radicchio on a plate, drizzle with balsamic reduction, and serve.

Special Summer Dishes

It wasn't easy to narrow down all the dishes I like to use in the summer. I just went for a variety of favorites that are unusual and elegant.

Grilled Herbed Corn on the Cob

Serves 6

Active time: 1 hour

Total time: 1 hour and 20 minutes

There are so many ways to dress up grilled corn with herbs from the garden. This one is my favorite.

2	heads of garlic
4	teaspoons extra-virgin olive oil
1	tablespoon Earth Balance "butter"
¼	cup chopped cilantro
¼	cup chopped tarragon
	Sea salt and freshly ground pepper
6	large ears of corn in the husks

1. Preheat the oven to 350°F.

2. Cut off the top third of each garlic head. Stand heads cut-side up on foil and drizzle with 1 teaspoon oil. Wrap the garlic in the foil and bake for about 1 hour, until very soft.

3. Squeeze the garlic into a bowl. Stir in Earth Balance "butter," cilantro, tarragon, and the remaining oil. Season with salt and pepper.

4. Light a grill. Peel back the corn husks, keeping them attached. Discard the silk. Spread the herbed garlic all over the corn. Fold the husks back over the corn and tie the tops with string.

5. Wrap corn in foil.

6. Grill the corn over moderate heat, turning, until the kernels feel tender, 15 minutes. Remove the foil. Grill the ears over moderately high heat, turning until the husks are nicely charred, 5 minutes, then serve.

Roast Tomatoes with Fennel and White Beans

Serves 8

Active time: 3 minutes
Total time: 55 minutes

This is a robust, filling dish that tastes especially good on a stormy night. You will need a skillet that can go in the oven. I love well-seasoned cast iron.

2   large fennel bulbs with fronds
¾   cup extra-virgin olive oil
2   teaspoons coarse sea salt, divided
2   pints whole grape tomatoes or cherry tomatoes
4   large sprigs fresh oregano
3   large garlic cloves, thinly sliced
¼   teaspoon red pepper flakes
1   teaspoon freshly ground black pepper
2   (15-ounce) cans cannellini (white kidney) beans, drained

1. Preheat oven to 425°F.

2. Chop enough fennel fronds to measure ½ cup.

3. Trim fennel bulbs and cut in half vertically. Cut each bulb half into ¼-inch wedges, leaving some core attached to each wedge.

4. Heat oil in a large ovenproof skillet over medium-high heat until very hot, about 3 minutes.

5. Add fennel wedges in a single layer; sprinkle with 1 teaspoon coarse sea salt. Cook until fennel begins to brown and soften, turning occasionally, 10 to 12 minutes.

6. Add tomatoes, oregano, garlic, and red pepper flakes; sprinkle with 1 teaspoon coarse sea salt and 1 teaspoon pepper. Fold together gently.

7. Transfer skillet to oven. Bake fennel and tomatoes until soft, stirring occasionally, about 30 minutes.

8. Mix in beans and 6 tablespoons chopped fennel fronds. Bake 5 minutes longer to heat through.

9. Transfer to a large shallow bowl.

10. Sprinkle with remaining chopped fronds. Serve warm or at room temperature.

Roast Summer Squashes

Serves 4
Active time: 5 minutes
Total time: 27 minutes

There are so many different squashes in my garden. This dish is a great way to use them. Though the recipe calls for yellow summer squash, feel free to mix it up.

- 4 yellow summer squash or mixed summer squashes, halved
- 2 zucchini, halved
- 2 tablespoons extra-virgin olive oil
  Sea salt and freshly ground black pepper
- ¼ cup chopped fresh flat-leaf parsley
- 2 tablespoons fresh lime juice

1. Preheat oven to 475°F.
2. To prepare squash and zucchini, brush with 2 tablespoons oil. Sprinkle with salt and pepper.
3. Arrange squash and zucchini cut-side down in a single layer on a rimmed baking sheet. Bake for 15 minutes, or until squash and zucchini are tender and lightly browned, turning after 7 minutes.
4. Combine parsley, lime juice, ¼ teaspoon salt and ¼ teaspoon pepper.
5. Sprinkle parsley mixture over the squash. Serve right away.

Zucchini Fritters

Serves 4
Active time: 10 minutes
Total time: 22 minutes

My friends just gobble these up. They are light, delicious, and good for you—so make extra!

- 1 pound zucchini (2 medium), coarsely grated
- 1 teaspoon coarse sea salt
- ¼ cup water
- 2 scallions, finely chopped
- ½ cup spelt or garbanzo flour
- ¼ teaspoon freshly ground pepper
- ½ cup canola oil

1. Place zucchini in a colander set in the sink and toss with salt; let drain 10 minutes. Press out as much liquid as possible.
2. In a large bowl, combine water, zucchini, scallions, flour, and pepper.
3. Heat oil in a large skillet over medium heat.
4. Cook fritters in two batches. Drop 6 mounds of batter (2 tablespoons each) into skillet; flatten slightly. Cook, turning once, until browned, 2 to 3 minutes.
5. Transfer fritters to a paper–towel–lined plate and sprinkle with salt. Repeat with remaining batter.

Tempeh Pot Pies

SERVES 6–9
ACTIVE TIME: 5 MINUTES
TOTAL TIME: 50 MINUTES

I'm not big on meat substitutes,
but I love these pot pies.

FOR FILLING:

2   tablespoons olive oil plus more for the pan
2   cups diced eggplant
1   8-ounce package tempeh,
    cut into ½-inch cubes
1   small yellow onion, chopped
1   stalk celery, thinly chopped
2   tablespoons balsamic vinegar
1   (15-ounce) can tomato sauce
½   teaspoon red pepper flakes
    Sea salt and freshly ground pepper to taste

FOR BISCUIT DOUGH:

1⅔ cups all-purpose flour
1   tablespoon baking powder
½   teaspoon salt
⅔   cup hemp milk
⅓   cup Earth Balance "butter," melted
    or canola oil

1. Preheat oven to 425°F.
2. Coat four to six individual ramekins with oil and set aside. You can also use a 9-inch square pan or a rectangular pan.
3. To make filling, steam eggplant and tempeh for 10 to 15 minutes, until eggplant is soft and translucent.

4. At the same time, add olive oil to a large-size sauté pan and cook onion and celery until soft, 3 to 5 minutes.
5. Add vinegar and sauté for 1 minute.
6. Add tomato sauce, red pepper flakes, and cooked tempeh and eggplant. Simmer for 10 minutes, stirring occasionally.
7. Prepare the biscuit dough. Place flour, baking powder, and salt in a mixing bowl and stir together.
8. Pour in hemp milk and Earth Balance "butter" or canola oil, and mix just until dry ingredients are evenly moistened. The dough should be lumpy and sticky, not smooth like cake batter.
9. Remove sauté pan from heat and season with salt and pepper to taste.
10. Divide filling evenly among prepared ramekins or transfer into baking pan.
11. Drop dough by small spoonfuls on top of each ramekin.
12. Carefully spread dough with back of a spoon, so it evenly covers filling.
13. Bake pot pies until crust is golden, about 15 minutes. Serve hot.

SUMMER SANDWICHES

Nothing takes the place of a delicious sandwich. By the pool, at a picnic, or in a lunch box, you just can't go wrong with a sandwich.

Pesto Panini

SERVES 4

TOTAL TIME: 40 MINUTES

This is, quite simply, the perfect summer sandwich.

FOR PESTO:

2 cups loosely packed fresh basil leaves

2 whole garlic cloves, peeled

¼ cup pine nuts

2 tablespoons olive oil

1 to 2 teaspoons fresh lemon juice

FOR PANINI:

3 zucchini, sliced and roasted or grilled

8 large slices Italian bread, such as ciabatta

1 medium-size red onion, sliced

1 or 2 medium-size tomatoes, sliced

1 ripe avocado, peeled and sliced

2 tablespoons balsamic vinegar

Sea salt and freshly ground black pepper to taste

Olive oil, for brushing

1. To make the pesto, combine basil, garlic, pine nuts, and salt in a food processor or blender. Mix until smooth.

2. Add oil and lemon juice and process until smooth. If not using immediately, store pesto mixture in a tightly covered container in the refrigerator for up to 2 days.

3. Grill or roast zucchini, 20 minutes.

4. To make panini, spread pesto on 4 slices of bread (about 2 tablespoons on each). Divide zucchini, onion, tomatoes, and avocado evenly on the bread.

5. Drizzle each with vinegar, and sprinkle on salt and pepper to taste.

6. Top each panino with remaining bread slices, lightly brush outside with a little olive oil, and press in a panini maker or place on a tabletop grill. Press until lightly browned and hot. You can cook the lightly oiled sandwiches in a skillet instead of grilling them, 5 minutes. Serve immediately.

Focaccia Flatbread with Caramelized Onions and Pears

SERVES 8
ACTIVE TIME: 25 MINUTES
TOTAL TIME: 1 HOUR AND 5 MINUTES

Caramelized onions are delicious with anything. Get ready for a treat when you combine them with pears.

- 5 tablespoons extra-virgin olive oil
- 1 large onion, thinly sliced
- 1 teaspoon light brown sugar (optional—I often leave it out)
- 1 package store-bought whole wheat pizza dough
- 1 teaspoon sea salt
- 1 large Bosc pear, cored and sliced

1. Preheat the oven to 450°F.
2. In a skillet, heat 1 tablespoon oil.
3. Add the onion, cover, and cook over moderate heat, stirring occasionally, for 10 minutes.
4. Add the sugar, cover, and cook, stirring occasionally, until browned, 10 minutes.
5. Oil a 9- by 13-inch rimmed baking sheet.
6. Transfer the dough to the sheet and press it down to fit. Dimple the dough all over with your fingers and drizzle with 2 tablespoons olive oil.
7. Let the dough rise until puffed, about 20 minutes.
8. Scatter the onions over the dough.
9. Arrange the pear over the onion.
10. Drizzle the remaining 2 tablespoons oil over the focaccia
11. Bake for 20 minutes, until golden.
12. Transfer to a rack to cool. Serve.

Hummus and Artichoke Sandwich

SERVES 4
TOTAL TIME: 25 MINUTES

This sandwich is filling without being heavy. It's packed with protein and energy.

- 1 (12-ounce) jar marinated baby artichoke hearts in oil
- 1 tablespoon oil from jar of artichokes
- 1 (15½-ounce) can chickpeas
- 1 teaspoon tahini
- ¼ cup extra-virgin olive oil
- 1 garlic clove
- 1 tablespoon fresh lemon juice
- ½ teaspoon salt
- ¼ teaspoon pepper
- ¼ cup water
- 4 slices country bread
- ¼ cup sliced pepperoncini peppers
- ¼ cup sun-dried tomatoes, chopped

1. Preheat oven to 400°F.
2. Drain artichokes, reserving 1 tablespoon of the oil. Toss artichokes with oil on a rimmed baking sheet and bake until dark brown, about 15 minutes.

3. For hummus, combine chickpeas, tahini, olive oil, garlic, lemon juice, salt, pepper, and water in a food processor; process until smooth. Add water to desired consistency.
4. Spread 2 tablespoons of hummus on a slice of country bread. Layer each slice evenly with artichokes, peppers, and sun-dried tomatoes.
5. Arrange open-face sandwiches on a baking sheet. Bake until warmed through, about 3 to 5 minutes.

Caesar Wraps

Serves 4
Total time: 30 minutes

You can use nori sheets instead of bread.

1 large head romaine lettuce, divided, with four large leaves reserved
1 cup halved cherry tomatoes
2 teaspoons dulse flakes (a nutritional powerhouse, made from sun-dried Atlantic seaweed)
1 celery stalk, finely chopped
  Dairy-free Caesar Dressing (recipe follows)
4 sheets untoasted nori or any kind of wrap you like
1 avocado, thinly sliced

1. Chop head of romaine and place in a large bowl.
2. Add tomatoes, dulse, and celery, and toss to mix.
3. Dress the mixture with 1 cup dressing.
4. Lay out a sheet of nori or wrap of your choice and top it with a leaf of romaine.
5. Pile ½ cup of the filling mixture on the bottom end of the wrap, and then layer a few avocado slices on top.
6. Starting at the bottom, fold the nori sheet and romaine over the filling and wrap it up, sealing the ends with a bit of water (as if making sushi). Repeat with remaining ingredients to make 4 wraps.

Caesar Dressing

Makes 1½ cups

½ cup cashews
¼ cup hemp seeds, shelled
¼ cup nutritional yeast (a cheese substitute)
¼ teaspoon salt
  Juice of 2 lemons
  Freshly ground black pepper to taste
3 pitted dates
1 teaspoon dulse flakes
¾ cup water
2 celery stalks, chopped

In a blender, combine all ingredients until completely smooth.

Focaccia Flatbread with Caramelized Onions and Pears at a summer dinner.

Guilt-Free Burgers

Here are some cruelty-free alternatives to America's favorite food. You can make them in advance and freeze them—so you will always have a fallback for unexpected guests or spontaneous get-togethers.

Black Bean Burgers

Serves 4
Total time: 40 minutes

Everyone loves these.

3   tablespoons olive oil
½   cup minced onion
1   garlic clove, minced
1½ cups cooked or 1 (15½-ounce) can black beans, drained and rinsed
1   tablespoon minced fresh parsley
½   cup dry unseasoned bread crumbs
¼   cup wheat gluten flour
1   teaspoon smoked paprika
½   teaspoon dried thyme
     Sea salt and freshly ground black pepper
4   whole wheat burger rolls, toasted and buttered with Earth Balance "butter"
4   lettuce leaves
1   ripe tomato, cut into ¼-inch slices

1. In a small skillet, heat 1 tablespoon of oil over medium heat. Add the onion and garlic and cook until softened, about 5 minutes.

2. Transfer the onion mixture to a food processor. Add the beans, parsley, bread crumbs, flour, paprika, thyme, and salt and pepper to taste. Process until well combined, leaving some texture.

3. Shape the mixture into 4 equal patties and refrigerate for 20 minutes.

4. In a large skillet, heat the remaining 2 tablespoons oil over medium heat. Add the burgers and cook until browned on both sides, turning once, about 5 minutes per side.

5. Toast rolls and spread with Earth Balance "butter."

6. Serve the burgers on the rolls with lettuce and tomato. The cooked burger patties can be frozen and reheated later.

Cashew Lentil Burgers

SERVES 6

TOTAL TIME: 45 MINUTES

This burger is packed with protein, and the cashews and lentils go so well together.

2 cups water

1 cup diced carrots (2 to 4 medium carrots)

½ cup red lentils, rinsed and picked through

½ teaspoon sea salt, plus more to taste

1 cup raw cashews

2 tablespoons olive oil

1 medium onion, chopped

1 garlic clove, minced

1 teaspoon curry powder

1 cup bread crumbs (more may be needed)

   Freshly ground black pepper to taste

6 (6-inch) whole wheat pita breads

   Lettuce, tomatoes, and Vegenaise, for toppings

1. Combine the water, carrots, lentils, and salt in a saucepan. Bring to a boil. Reduce the heat to low, then cover and simmer until the lentils are tender and broken down, 12 to 14 minutes.

2. Drain in a colander, pressing out the excess liquid.

3. Transfer to a bowl and let cool to room temperature, about 20 minutes.

4. Toast the cashews in a small dry skillet over medium-low heat or in the toaster oven until golden and fragrant. Let cool completely.

5. Heat 1 tablespoon oil in a large sauté pan over medium heat. Add the onion and cook, stirring, until softened, about 7 minutes.

6. Add the garlic and curry powder and cook, stirring, for 1 minute. Remove from the heat and let cool.

7. Place the cooled cashews in a food processor and pulse until finely chopped. Add the lentils and the onion mixture; pulse until the mixture is cohesive but still somewhat textured.

8. Transfer to a bowl and add enough bread crumbs to create a consistency that enables you to form patties. Season with salt and pepper to taste. With moist hands, form the mixture into six ½-inch-thick patties.

9. Heat the remaining 1 tablespoon oil in a large sauté pan over medium heat, and cook the patties until evenly browned and heated through, about 4 minutes on each side.

10. Serve in warmed pitas with lettuce, tomatoes, and Vegenaise. These burgers can be frozen before cooking.

Chickpea Patties with Salad

SERVES 8

TOTAL TIME: 10 MINUTES

This is a nice twist on falafel.

- 1 (15½-ounce) can chickpeas, drained and rinsed
- ½ cup fresh flat-leaf parsley
- 1 garlic clove, chopped
- ¼ teaspoon ground cumin
- ½ teaspoon sea salt, divided
- ½ teaspoon freshly ground black pepper, divided
- 2 tablespoons whole wheat, spelt, or garbanzo flour
- 2 tablespoons olive oil
- ½ cup Vegenaise
- 3 tablespoons fresh lemon juice
- 8 cups mixed greens
- 1 cup grape tomatoes
- ½ small red onion, thinly sliced

1. In a food processor, pulse the chickpeas, parsley, garlic, cumin, and ¼ teaspoon each salt and pepper just until coarsely chopped and the mixture comes together when gently squeezed.

2. Form into eight ½-inch-thick patties and coat with the flour, tapping off excess.

3. Heat oil in a nonstick skillet over medium-high heat. Cook the patties, turning carefully, until golden brown, 2 to 3 minutes per side.

4. In a small bowl, whisk the Veganaise, lemon juice, and ¼ teaspoon each salt and pepper.

5. Put chickpea patties on a platter with the greens, tomatoes, onion, and dressing on the side.

Chickpea Patties with Salad, grilled pita, and Vegenaise on the side.

Fresh Sliced Yellow and White Peaches with Mint and Lemon

SERVES 6

TOTAL TIME: 10 MINUTES

What signifies summer more than peaches? They are so sweet and juicy you don't have to fuss with them to make a memorable dessert.

- 2 pounds yellow and white peaches
- ¼ cup loosely chopped mint
  Juice of 1 small lemon (1½ teaspoons)

Slice peaches and put in a serving bowl. Add mint and lemon juice and toss.

Berry Crumble

I usually eat more berries as I'm picking them as end up in the bowl. But it's worth postponing gratification and to wait for this crumble.

BERRY FILLING:
- 4 pints mixed berries
- ½ cup orange juice
- 1 cup cane sugar
- 2 tablespoons cornstarch

CRUMBLE TOPPING:
- 1 cup all-purpose flour
- 1 cup quick-cooking rolled oats
- ¼ cup cane sugar
- 6 ounces Earth Balance "butter," chilled and diced
- 1 teaspoon salt

1. Preheat the oven to 350°F.

2. Lightly grease a shallow baking dish that has a capacity to hold about 3 quarts and is 2 to 3 inches deep.

3. In a mixing bowl, prepare the berry filling by tossing together the berries, orange juice, sugar, and cornstarch. Leave at room temperature for 15 minutes.

4. Prepare the crumble topping. In another mixing bowl, combine the flour, oats, sugar, and salt. Add the Earth Balance "butter". Mixing with your hands, make clumps of all sizes.

5. Stir the berry mixture and pour into your prepared baking dish; it should be about three-quarters full. With your hands, crumble the topping evenly over the filling.

6. Bake in the preheated oven until golden brown and bubbling, 20 to 25 minutes. Serve hot, and add ice cream! *So good!*

Tomato Tarte Tatin

SERVES 8

ACTIVE TIME: 30 MINUTES

TOTAL TIME: 1 HOUR AND 30 MINUTES

This dessert will surprise your friends.
It is a nice twist on a French classic.

1¾ pounds (8 large) plum tomatoes
  3 tablespoons Earth Balance "butter"
     at room temperature
1¼ cups cane sugar
  1 teaspoon vanilla extract
  1 sheet dairy-free phyllo dough
     (half of a 17.3-ounce package), thawed,
     corners cut off to make a very rough
     9- to 10-inch round
     Dairy-free whipped cream

1. Preheat oven to 425°F

2. Bring a large saucepan of water to boil.

3. Cut shallow X in bottom of each tomato.

4. Add 4 tomatoes to boiling water. Blanch tomatoes just until skins at X begin to peel back, 15 to 30 seconds.

5. Using a slotted spoon, transfer blanched tomatoes to a bowl of ice water to cool quickly. Repeat with remaining tomatoes.

6. Peel tomatoes, cut out cores, halve lengthwise, and remove seeds.

7. Spread Earth Balance "butter" over bottom of 9½-inch-diameter, 2- to 3-inch-deep ovenproof skillet (preferably cast iron).

8. Sprinkle cane sugar over Earth Balance "butter."

9. Arrange tomato halves, rounded-side down and close together, in concentric circles in skillet to fill completely.

10. Place skillet over medium heat. Cook until sugar and butter are reduced to thickly bubbling, deep amber syrup (about ¼ inch deep in bottom of skillet), moving tomatoes occasionally to prevent burning, about 25 minutes.

11. Remove skillet from heat and immediately drizzle vanilla over tomatoes.

12. Top with pastry round. Using a knife, tuck edges of pastry around tomatoes. Cut 2 or 3 small slits in pastry.

13. Place skillet in oven and bake tart until pastry is deep golden brown, about 24 minutes.

14. Remove tart from oven and let cool in skillet 10 minutes. Cut around sides of skillet to loosen pastry.

15. Place a large platter over skillet. Using oven mitts as an aid, hold skillet and platter firmly together and invert over platter, allowing tart to settle onto platter.

16. Carefully lift off skillet. Rearrange any tomato halves that may have become dislodged.

17. Serve tart warm or at room temperature with dairy-free whipped cream.

PART 4

FALL

A pillar of the rose garden.

all is my favorite time of year. I was born on Thanksgiving Day, and we always celebrated my birthday on Thanksgiving. There are no turkeys or pigs at my table! The change in the light in late August is the first sign that summer is winding down. As the days shorten, autumn seems like a drowsy time before a well-deserved nap for Mother Nature. The changing of the leaves—the vibrant oranges, reds, and yellows—is a majestic finale. What a way to go!

The geese fly by in formation, off to warmer climates. Squirrels, chipmunks, deer, and raccoons get fat and furry, ready for the cold weather ahead. The fall is a time for long, invigorating walks.

Autumn calls for heartier dishes. I love to roast broccoli, brussels sprouts, cauliflower, winter squash, yams, and kale—the house smells so good. For dessert, apple crumbles, plum tarts, and pumpkin pies. I love to pick pumpkins and carve them for Halloween and do a yummy buffet on Sunday, watch a great game, or just relax. We grow dahlias the size of dinner plates and bushes of daisies and asters.

When I have guests at Templeton in the fall, they generally wake up later than in the summer, maybe because the days are beginning to get shorter and the light has changed. The cool weather makes us want to stay in bed longer! When they surface, they are always

*My mother gave me this stirrup cup
for my birthday one Thanksgiving.
I cherish it. It was her mother's.
It's always at my place at the table so
everyone knows where I'm sitting.*

happy to have a hearty breakfast waiting for them. I like to have a buffet, so that there is something for everyone.

When most people think of breakfast, the first thing that comes to mind is bacon and eggs. Not at my house! No one ever misses them, and no one ever leaves hungry. These recipes prove how easy it is to prepare a delicious breakfast spread without using eggs, milk, and other animal products.

Aside from the amazing falling leaves, beautiful flowers are still blooming in the fall. The following list names some of the outstanding flowers of fall.

When my perennial beds fill up with chrysanthemums in the fall, I harvest them and drop groups of five into little zinc cubes to line the dining room table. Any small, low container will do. If my mums look puny that fall, I sometimes purchase potted mums and cut from those instead of my garden, or even grab some from the grocery store.

MARGOT SHAW
Editor, Flower *magazine*

FALL FLOWERS Aster • Burning bush • Chrysanthemum • Cosmos Dahlia • Gerber daisy • Gourds Hosta • Monkshood • Ornamental kale • Ornamental cabbage • Queen Anne's lace • Roses • Yarrow • Zinnia

HEARTY FALL BREAKFAST

MENU

Pecan Waffles

French Toast

Faux Buttermilk Pancakes

Raspberry Muffins

Cinnamon Muffins

Debra's Granola

Breakfast Quinoa

Pecan Waffles

SERVES 4

TOTAL TIME: 30 MINUTES

I love antique waffle irons, and we all love waffles! Make sure the maple syrup is warmed, and the Earth Balance "butter" melted. The pecans add extra flavor and crunch.

1¾ cups all-purpose flour
⅓ cup coarsely ground pecans
1 tablespoon baking powder
½ teaspoon salt
1½ cups hemp or soy milk
3 tablespoons pure maple syrup
3 tablespoons Earth Balance "butter," melted

1. Oil the waffle iron lightly and preheat it. Preheat the oven to 225°F.
2. In a large bowl, combine the flour, pecans, baking powder, and salt. Set aside.
3. In a medium bowl, whisk together the hemp or soy milk, maple syrup, and Earth Balance "butter." Add the wet ingredients to the dry ingredients and blend with a few swift strokes, mixing until just combined.
4. Ladle ½ to 1 cup of the batter (depending on the instructions with your waffle iron) onto the hot waffle iron. Cook until done, 3 to 5 minutes for most waffle irons.
5. Transfer the cooked waffles to a heat-proof platter and keep warm in the oven while cooking the rest of the waffles.

French Toast

SERVES 4

TOTAL TIME: 15 TO 20 MINUTES

French toast is great comfort food and is a good way to use day-old bread. Remember to warm the maple syrup so that the Earth Balance "butter" melts.

1 (12-ounce) package firm silken tofu, drained
1½ cups hemp or soy milk
2 tablespoons cornstarch
1 tablespoon canola oil
1 teaspoon cane sugar
1½ teaspoons pure vanilla extract
¼ teaspoon salt
8 slices day-old Italian bread
 Canola oil, for frying

1. Preheat the oven to 225°F.
2. In a blender or food processor, combine the tofu, hemp or soy milk, cornstarch, oil, sugar, vanilla, and salt, and blend until smooth.
3. Pour the batter into a shallow bowl and dip the bread in the batter, turning to coat both sides.
4. On a griddle or large skillet, heat a thin layer of oil over medium heat.
5. Place the French toast on the hot griddle and cook until golden brown on both sides, turning once, 3 to 4 minutes per side.

6. Transfer the cooked French toast to a heatproof platter and keep warm in the oven while cooking the rest.

Faux Buttermilk Pancakes

<small>MAKES 6 MEDIUM PANCAKES</small>
<small>TOTAL TIME: 15 MINUTES</small>

Who doesn't love a pancake? Children love silver dollar pancakes because they are just their size, and adults love them because they are a healthy indulgence. They taste even better if you heat the maple syrup and melt the "butter."

1 cup all-purpose flour
1 cup plus 1 to 4 tablespoons hemp or soy milk
1 heaping tablespoon soy flour
1½ teaspoons baking powder
    Pinch of sea salt

OPTIONAL:
½ to 1 cup blueberries
2 ripe bananas, mashed, and ¼ cup chopped walnuts
½ cup chopped apples and 1 teaspoon cinnamon

1. Whisk flour, hemp or soy milk, soy flour, and salt together in a large bowl until no lumps remain. Gently fold in optional ingredients. Batter will be thick. If it is too thick to handle (humidity affects consistency), add more hemp or soy milk, 1 tablespoon at a time.
2. Cook on an oiled griddle or nonstick pan over medium-high heat until you start to see bubbles appearing. At this point, flip pancake and cook other side until golden brown.

Raspberry Muffins

<small>MAKES 12 MUFFINS</small>
<small>TOTAL TIME: 30 MINUTES</small>

Eat these colorful muffins when they are warm. They taste like a compote. You can freeze them if there are ever any left over.

1 (6-ounce) container vanilla or plain nondairy yogurt
½ cup hemp milk
3 tablespoons canola oil
1½ cups all-purpose or whole wheat pastry flour
¼ cup cane sugar
2½ teaspoons baking powder
¼ teaspoon salt
1 tablespoon apple cider vinegar
1 cup fresh raspberries or 9 ounces frozen

1. Preheat the oven to 400°F.
2. Lightly grease a 12-cup muffin tin or line with paper or silicone cupcake liners.
3. In a large bowl, mix together the yogurt, milk, and oil.

Raspberry Muffins, Cinnamon Muffins, Debra's Granola, Pecan Waffles with hot maple syrup and melted Earth Balance "butter". Who isn't happy to eat this! The tiger in the background is made of wood and I found him at a swap meet. And the trophy, The Hurlingham Cup, my Dad won in 1936. For buffets I use all the trophies my family has won over the years. I think it's important to use everything!

4. In a separate bowl, stir together the flour, sugar, baking powder, and salt.

5. Add the wet ingredients to the dry and mix until just blended.

6. Stir in the apple cider vinegar.

7. Gently fold in the raspberries. Spoon the batter evenly into the prepared muffin cups.

8. Bake for 20 to 25 minutes, or until the top springs back when lightly touched.

9. Cool the muffins in the tin on a wire rack.

Cinnamon Muffins

MAKES 12 MUFFINS

ACTIVE TIME: 35 MINUTES

TOTAL TIME: 2 HOURS AND 35 MINUTES

The crunchy, yummy topping makes this muffin. The smell of cinnamon when they are baking warms the whole house.

CRUNCH TOPPING:

¾ cup packed light brown sugar

⅔ cup organic whole wheat or all-purpose flour

2 tablespoons ground cinnamon

6 tablespoons Earth Balance "butter"

1 tablespoon apple cider vinegar

FOR MUFFINS:

½ cup canola oil

½ cup cane sugar

¼ cup applesauce

¼ cup hemp milk

½ cup dairy-free sour cream

1 teaspoon pure vanilla extract

2 cups whole wheat or all-purpose flour

1 teaspoon baking powder

½ teaspoon baking soda

1 teaspoon salt

Pinch of ground nutmeg

CRUNCH TOPPING:

1. Preheat the oven to 350°F.

2. In a medium bowl, combine the brown sugar, flour, and cinnamon.

3. Using a pastry cutter or your fingers, crumble in the Earth Balance "butter" until the mixed ingredients resemble pea-size lumps. Transfer the mixture to a baking sheet and bake for 7 to 8 minutes, until slightly golden.

4. Remove from the oven and place the pan on a cooling rack for 2 hours.

5. Stir in 1 tablespoon of apple cider vinegar.

6. Break the crumb mixture apart so the crumble is a little bigger than a pea. Set aside in a bowl.

MUFFINS

1. Preheat oven to 350°F.
2. Lightly oil a muffin tin.
3. In a large bowl, combine the oil, sugar, applesauce, hemp milk, dairy-free sour cream, and vanilla. Whisk together until the sugar is dissolved and ingredients are combined.
4. In a medium bowl, whisk together the flour, baking powder, baking soda, salt, and nutmeg.
5. Add the dry mixture to the wet ingredients.
6. Add 1¼ cups of the crunch mixture. Stir gently to combine, but don't overmix.
7. Transfer the batter to the muffin tin, filling the cups to almost full.
8. Sprinkle 1 tablespoon of the remaining crunch mixture onto each muffin.
9. Bake 25 to 30 minutes, or until golden brown.
10. Cool in the pan for 5 minutes, then transfer to a rack to finish cooling.

Debra's Granola

SERVES 10–12
TOTAL TIME: 25 MINUTES

Debra Cindrich makes the best granola ever. I eat it anytime, anywhere—for breakfast, lunch, dinner, and a snack. It's not too sweet.

5	cups oats
1	cup sunflower or pumpkin seeds
¾	cup raw sesame seeds
1	cup wheat germ
2	cups shredded coconut
1½	cups pecan halves, chopped
1½	cups chopped walnuts
¾	teaspoon salt
1	tablespoon cinnamon
1	teaspoon vanilla
¾	cup maple syrup
1	cup canola oil

1. Preheat oven to 350°F.
2. Mix the oats, sunflower or pumpkin seeds, sesame seeds, wheat germ, coconut, pecans, walnuts, salt, and cinnamon.
3. Once all are combined add the vanilla, maple syrup, and canola oil. Mix thoroughly and lay out on a cookie sheet.
4. Bake for 10 minutes, remove, and stir up the mixture, then return to oven for 10 minutes. If you keep granola in a tightly sealed container, it will stay fresh for 2 weeks.

Breakfast Quinoa

Serves 4
Total time: 20 minutes

This porridge is a nice switch from oatmeal. It sticks to your ribs and is terrific comfort food, especially if you and your guests have had too much to drink the night before.

1 cup red quinoa, rinsed
1 tablespoon extra-virgin olive oil
¼ cup slivered almonds
½ cup dried apricots, cut into ½-inch pieces
2 tablespoons pure maple syrup
½ teaspoon ground cinnamon

1. In a small saucepan, cover the quinoa with water and bring to a boil. Cover and cook over low heat until the water has been absorbed and the quinoa is tender, about 15 minutes. Lightly fluff the quinoa with a fork and cover it again.
2. In a medium skillet, heat the olive oil (can be roasted instead, with no oil). Add the almonds and cook over moderate heat, stirring a few times, until golden brown, about 2 minutes. Add the apricots and cinnamon and stir well until heated through.
3. Add the quinoa to the skillet and stir to incorporate the almonds and apricots. Stir in maple syrup.

Fall is harvesting time. We are busy making pesto with the last of the basil, steaming or sautéing eggplant and zucchini, and roasting tomatoes for the freezer to get us through the winter months. I love autumn vegetables—they are more substantial than spring and summer produce, just what we need as the days get shorter and the temperature cools.

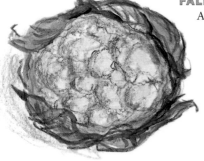

FALL VEGETABLES
Acorn squash • Broccoli • Broccoli rabe • Brussels sprouts • Buttercup squash • Butternut squash • Cauliflower • Celery • Chard • Collard greens • Daikon radish • Eggplant • Fennel • Jerusalem artichoke Kale • Mushrooms • Radicchio • Spinach • Sweet potatoes Turnips • Winter squash

FALL FRUITS
Apples • Cranberries • Grapes • Oranges • Pears • Persimmons Pomegranates • Pumpkins • Quince • Tangerines

Mulled Cider

SERVES 8
TOTAL TIME: 45 MINUTES

We have a small apple orchard at Templeton, but I pick different fruits at other orchards. I always take home a gallon of fresh-pressed apple cider to make this recipe. Nothing makes the house smell better than mulled cider simmering away on the stove. Sometimes I'll take a thermos of it with me when I go for a walk. Keeps me warm.

1 gallon apple cider
¾ cup dry white wine, such as Chardonnay
¼ cup honey
2 quince, peeled, cored and finely chopped
1 (4-inch) sprig rosemary
2 (3- to 4-inch) sticks cinnamon, broken
4 cloves
1 star anise pod
½ teaspoon grated lemon peel

1. Combine the cider, wine, honey, quince, rosemary, cinnamon, cloves, star anise, and lemon peel in a large saucepan, and simmer over low heat for 45 minutes.
2. Strain the mulled cider and discard the solids.
3. Serve the mulled cider warm.

Guacamole Hummus

SERVES 8
TOTAL TIME: 5 MINUTES

Chickpeas make this dip a little heavier for fall.

1 (15½-ounce) can chickpeas, rinsed and drained
3 cups fresh cilantro
1 garlic clove, chopped
1 ripe avocado, roughly chopped
3 tablespoons extra-virgin olive oil
1 teaspoon fresh lemon juice
  Coarse sea salt and freshly ground black pepper
  Lemon wedges and tortilla chips or raw vegetable crudités, for serving

1. In a food processor, combine chickpeas, cilantro, garlic, and avocado. Process until finely chopped.
2. With machine running, add olive oil in a slow, steady stream, then the fresh lemon juice.
3. Add water, 1 tablespoon at a time, until mixture is smooth.
4. Season with sea salt and freshly ground black pepper to taste.

Mushroom Pâté. The perfect start for any cold day. I found this rabbit casserole at a flea market in Paris and carried it home. It's one of my favorite things to serve pâtés and dips in. My mother and I are in the background having fun at a party.

Mushroom Pâté

MAKES ABOUT 2 CUPS

TOTAL TIME: 12 MINUTES

Mushrooms give this pâté a delicious, nutty flavor, perfect for fall.

1 tablespoon olive oil

½ cup chopped onion

1 garlic clove, minced

2 cups white mushrooms, thinly sliced

½ teaspoon dried savory

Sea salt and freshly ground black pepper

½ cup raw cashews

Chopped fresh parsley, for garnish

1. In a large skillet, heat the oil over medium heat.

2. Add the onion and garlic, cover, and cook until softened, about 5 minutes.

3. Add the mushrooms and savory. Add salt and pepper to taste.

4. Cook, uncovered, stirring occasionally, until the mushrooms are soft and the

Eggplant Dip.

liquid is evaporated, about 5 minutes. Set aside to cool.

5. In a food processor, grind the cashews to a fine powder.

6. Add the cooled mushroom mixture and process until smooth.

7. Spoon the pâté into a small crock or serving bowl. Smooth the top and sprinkle with parsley.

8. Cover and refrigerate for at least 1 hour before serving.

Eggplant Dip

SERVES 12
ACTIVE TIME: 37 MINUTES
TOTAL TIME: 2 HOURS

Eggplant is one of my all-time favorite vegetables. I use this dip for everything— in a sandwich, a wrap, on a burger, pasta, veggies, or on top of a bed of lettuce.

3 medium eggplants (3 pounds)
¼ cup plus 1 tablespoon extra-virgin olive oil

1 teaspoon garlic, minced or finely grated
3 cloves
2 tablespoons chopped parsley
  Coarse sea salt

1. Preheat oven to 400°F.
2. Roast eggplants on a baking sheet until collapsed and very tender, about 1 hour and 15 minutes.
3. Remove from oven and let stand until cool enough to handle, about 20 minutes.
4. Peel, discard skins, and transfer flesh to a colander. Let drain for 15 minutes.
5. Finely chop eggplant and transfer to a bowl.
6. Stir in 3 tablespoons oil, minced garlic, cloves, parsley, and 1½ teaspoons salt.
7. Heat remaining 2 tablespoons oil and the sliced garlic in a skillet over medium heat until garlic is golden, 6 to 7 minutes.
8. Drizzle garlic-oil over dip and garnish with garlic chips.

Couscous Dolmas

MAKES ABOUT 20
TOTAL TIME: 25 MINUTES

Dolma means "stuffed thing" in Turkish. For this dish, grape leaves are stuffed with a simple vegan filling. The dolmas can be made the day before and served cold or at room temperature.

2 tablespoons olive oil
½ cup minced onion
1 cup couscous
1½ cups vegetable broth
¼ cup chopped cashews
2 tablespoons minced fresh parsley
  Sea salt and freshly ground black pepper
1 (16-ounce) jar grape leaves, drained, rinsed, and patted dry
2 tablespoons fresh lemon juice

1. In a medium saucepan, heat 1 tablespoon oil over medium heat.
2. Add the onion, cover, and cook until softened, about 5 minutes.
3. Add the couscous and stir in the broth, cashews, parsley, and salt and pepper to taste.
4. Cover and remove from heat. Set aside for 5 minutes.
5. Stir in lemon juice.
6. Trim the stems from the grape leaves.
7. Place one grape leaf at a time on a cutting board, shiny side down.
8. Place 1 tablespoon of the couscous mixture near the stem end and fold the sides of the leaf over the filling.
9. Beginning at the stem end, roll up the leaf firmly into a neat roll.
10. Repeat with the remaining ingredients and grape leaves.

Sweet Potato Watercress Salad. This is an old silver and wood salad bowl with a ceramic inlay. One of my favorites!

Sweet Potato Watercress Salad

SERVES 4
ACTIVE TIME: 15 MINUTES
TOTAL TIME: 50 MINUTES

Watercress is Mother Nature's version of a multivitamin, a superfood.

2 medium sweet potatoes, peeled and cut into 2-inch-long matchsticks (about 1 pound)

3 tablespoons plus ½ teaspoon olive oil

Coarse sea salt and freshly ground black pepper

½ cup walnuts, toasted

¼ teaspoon cayenne pepper

2 tablespoons fresh lemon juice

2 bunches watercress, stems trimmed, (about 12 ounces)

1. Preheat oven to 450°F, with racks on upper and lower thirds.

2. On a rimmed baking sheet, toss sweet potatoes with 1 tablespoon oil; season with salt and pepper.

3. Roast on upper rack until tender, 30 to 35 minutes, tossing halfway through.

4. On another rimmed baking sheet, toss walnuts with cayenne and ½ teaspoon oil.

5. Bake on lower rack until golden, 6 minutes.

6. In a medium bowl, whisk together lemon juice and remaining 2 tablespoons oil; season with salt and pepper.

7. Add watercress and toss to combine.

8. Serve topped with sweet potatoes and toasted walnuts.

Apple Beet Salad

SERVES 8

ACTIVE TIME: 20 MINUTES

TOTAL TIME: 2 HOURS

This salad is a great way to use all those apples you take home from the farm stand or farmers' market. It is sweet and crunchy, and great with grain dishes and pasta.

4 large beets (2½ pounds)
  (you can use different color beets)

5 sprigs thyme

½ cup extra-virgin olive oil, plus more
  for drizzling
  Sea salt and freshly ground black pepper

¼ cup apple cider vinegar

1 teaspoon Dijon mustard

2 tablespoons prepared horseradish

⅓ cup salted pistachios, chopped

1 green apple, thinly sliced

1. Preheat oven to 375°F.

2. In a baking dish, lightly drizzle the beets and thyme with olive oil.

3. Season with salt and pepper.

4. Cover with foil and roast until beets are tender, about 1 hour and 45 minutes.

5. Let cool, then peel the beets and cut them into ¾-inch dice or quarters.

6. In a large bowl, whisk the vinegar with the mustard.

7. Whisk in the remaining olive oil until emulsified.

8. Add the horseradish and season with salt and pepper.

9. Toss dressing with the beets and pistachios.

10. Transfer the beets to a platter, top with the apple, and serve.

Porcini Pappardelle with Pistachios

SERVES 6

TOTAL TIME: 45 MINUTES

I use pappardelle, a wide, flat pasta, because it holds the sauce well. This is very filling and has an added crunch.

- 6   tablespoons Earth Balance "butter"
- 1   large red onion, cut into ¾-inch dice
- 1   pound fresh porcini or cremini mushrooms, thinly sliced
     Sea salt and freshly ground black pepper
- 1   shallot, minced
- 1   garlic clove, thinly sliced
- 2   cups vegetable stock
- 2   tablespoons flat-leaf parsley, chopped
- ½   cup unsalted roasted pistachios
- 1   small chile, such as red Thai chile, seeded and minced
- 1   pound pappardelle, preferably fresh
- 2   tablespoons extra-virgin olive oil

1. Put on a large pot of salted water to boil for the pasta.

2. In a large, deep skillet, melt 4 tablespoons of Earth Balance "butter."

3. Add the onion and cook over low heat, stirring occasionally, until softened but not browned, about 10 minutes.

4. Using a slotted spoon, transfer the onion to a bowl; leave as much of the "butter" in the pan as possible.

5. Add the mushrooms to the skillet, season with salt and pepper, and cook over high heat, stirring occasionally, until the liquid is evaporated and the mushrooms are golden, about 8 minutes.

6. Stir in the shallot and garlic and cook for 1 minute.

7. Return the onion to the skillet. Add the vegetable stock and parsley and simmer over moderately high heat until the liquid is reduced to ¼ cup, about 8 minutes.

8. Add the remaining 2 tablespoons "butter" along with the pistachios and chile and stir until the "butter" is melted. Season with salt and pepper.

9. Cook the pappardelle in a large pot of boiling salted water until al dente.

10. Drain the pasta, reserving ½ cup of the cooking water.

11. Add the pappardelle to the skillet along with the reserved cooking water and the olive oil.

12. Cook over moderately high heat, tossing, until the pasta is coated with a thick sauce, about 2 minutes.

13. Transfer to bowls and serve.

Broccoli Rabe Orecchiette. I inherited the set of dishes with my family crest. I use it only for sit-down dinners, mostly Christmas Eve. It's so simple, yet elegant, which I love.

Broccoli Rabe Orecchiette

SERVES 4
ACTIVE TIME: 15 MINUTES
TOTAL TIME: 45 MINUTES

The lemon cuts the bitterness of the broccoli rabe. The simple ingredients make the flavors stand out—absolutely delicious. It can be served as a main course or side dish.

Coarse sea salt

¾ pound orecchiette or other small pasta shapes

1 bunch broccoli rabe, trimmed and cut into 1½-inch pieces, (about 1 pound)

¼ cup extra-virgin olive oil

4 garlic cloves, thinly sliced

½ teaspoon red pepper flakes

Freshly ground black pepper

1 tablespoon fresh oregano leaves, for serving

2–3 tablespoons fresh lemon juice, for serving

1. In a large pot of boiling salted water, cook pasta according to package directions, adding broccoli rabe 4 minutes before end of cooking.
2. Meanwhile, in a small saucepan, heat oil, garlic, and red pepper flakes over medium heat until garlic begins to sizzle, 2 minutes.
3. Drain pasta and broccoli rabe and return to pot.
4. Add oil mixture and toss to coat; season to taste with salt and pepper.
5. To serve, sprinkle oregano over pasta and drizzle with lemon juice.

Spaghetti with Cauliflower

SERVES 4 TO 6

ACTIVE TIME: 30 MINUTES

I can't get enough cauliflower. You can throw this together in no time and serve it with a salad. Voilà—it's a delicious dinner.

    5   tablespoons extra-virgin olive oil
    ¼   cup panko (Japanese bread crumbs)
    1   medium onion, halved and thinly sliced
    1   (1½-pound) head cauliflower, cut into 1-inch florets
    2   large garlic cloves, minced
    3   cups vegetable broth
    ½   cup prepared tomato sauce
    1   tablespoon tomato paste
    1   pound spaghetti

    Sea salt and freshly ground black pepper
    ¼   cup pine nuts, toasted

1. Bring a large pot of water to a boil.
2. In a large, deep skillet, heat 2 tablespoons olive oil.
3. Add the panko and toast until golden, about 1 minute. Transfer to a plate.
4. Wipe out the skillet and heat the remaining 3 tablespoons oil. Add the onion and cook until translucent, 3 minutes.
5. Add the cauliflower and garlic and cook for 1 minute.
6. Add the broth, tomato sauce, and tomato paste, and bring to a simmer. Cover partially and cook until the cauliflower is just tender, 10 minutes.
7. While cauliflower is cooking, salt the boiling water and cook spaghetti according to package directions.
8. Drain the spaghetti, add to the cauliflower, and toss to coat.
9. Season with salt and pepper and cook over moderate heat, tossing, until sauce thickens, about 3 minutes.
10. Transfer the spaghetti to bowls, garnish with the pine nuts and panko, and serve.

Winter Squash with Bulgur

SERVES 4 TO 6
ACTIVE TIME: 40 MINUTES
TOTAL TIME: 3 HOURS AND 40 MINUTES–
4 HOURS AND 40 MINUTES

I always look forward to fall and winter squash. The mix of winter squash and bulgur makes this dish look like fall.

- 2 pounds banana squash, red kuri, or pumpkin (about 3 cups)
- ¼ teaspoon salt
- 1 medium onion, diced
- ⅓ cup extra-virgin olive oil
- 1 cup large-grain bulgur
- ½ teaspoon ground cinnamon
- ¼ teaspoon finely ground black pepper
  Salt

1. Peel and finely dice the squash.
2. Put a small pot of water on to boil, about 8 minutes.
3. In a wide skillet, sauté the onion and squash in the olive oil until soft and golden.
4. Place the bulgur in a fine sieve. Shake to remove any dust but do not wash.
5. Add the bulgur and 1½ cups boiling water to the skillet, bring to a boil, stir once, cover the pan, lower the heat, and cook 20 minutes, or until the liquid has been absorbed.

6. Stir in the cinnamon, black pepper, and salt to taste. Remove from the heat and let stand 5 minutes before serving.

Oven Fries

SERVES 6
ACTIVE TIME: 10 MINUTES
TOTAL TIME: 40 MINUTES

Roasted potatoes are a classic favorite. I adore garlic, and I think it makes this dish especially delicious.

- 3 large Yukon Gold potatoes, halved lengthwise and cut into ½-inch-thick wedges (1¾ pounds)
- 8 unpeeled garlic cloves
- 3 tablespoons extra-virgin olive oil
  Sea salt and freshly ground black pepper
- ¼ cup parsley leaves

1. Preheat the oven to 425°F.
2. On a large rimmed baking sheet, toss the potatoes and garlic cloves with the olive oil.
3. Spread the potatoes in an even layer, cut-sides down. Season with salt and pepper.
4. Bake for about 30 minutes, or until the potatoes are browned on the bottom and very crisp.
5. Peel the garlic cloves.
6. Transfer the potatoes and garlic to a platter, sprinkle with parsley leaves, and serve.

Roast Cauliflower with Turmeric

SERVES 4–6
TOTAL TIME: 50 MINUTES

Fall is a great time for roasting. This dish is spicy and colorful. It looks great on a plate.

- 1 teaspoon coriander seeds
- ½ teaspoon white peppercorns
- ¼ cup extra-virgin olive oil
- 1 tablespoon minced garlic
- 2 teaspoons ground turmeric
- ½ teaspoon red pepper flakes
- 1 (3-pound) head of cauliflower, cored and separated into 1-inch florets
  Sea salt
- 1 medium shallot, thinly sliced and separated into rings
- ¼ cup chopped cilantro

1. Preheat oven to 400°F.
2. In a small skillet, toast the coriander seeds and peppercorns over moderately high heat until fragrant, about 30 seconds.
3. Transfer to a spice grinder and let cool completely, 20 minutes.
4. Grind the spices to a powder and transfer to a small bowl.
5. Stir in the olive oil, garlic, turmeric, and red pepper flakes.
6. On a large rimmed baking sheet, drizzle the cauliflower with the olive oil mixture and toss to coat. Season with salt.
7. Roast for 25 minutes, until the cauliflower is tender.
8. Scrape the cauliflower into a serving bowl. Add the shallot rings and cilantro and toss well.
9. Serve hot or warm.

Cauliflower Puree

SERVES 12
ACTIVE TIME: 50 MINUTES
TOTAL TIME: 1 HOUR AND 20 MINUTES

I told you I love cauliflower—as you can tell by how many recipes I have for it. Cooked this way, cauliflower is a great low-calorie substitute for mashed potatoes.

- 2 (2-pound) heads of cauliflower, cored and separated into 2-inch florets
- ½ cup hemp milk
- 1½ sticks Earth Balance "butter"
  Sea salt
  Cayenne pepper

1. Preheat the oven to 325°F.
2. In a large pot of boiling salted water, cook the cauliflower florets until tender, about 7 minutes. Drain well.
3. Spread the cauliflower on a large rimmed baking sheet. Bake for 5 minutes to dry it out.
4. Combine the hemp milk with the Earth Balance "butter" in a small saucepan

and bring to a simmer over moderate heat, just until the "butter" is melted.

5. Working in batches, puree the cauliflower in a blender with the warm cream mixture.

6. Transfer the puree to a medium-size microwave-safe bowl.

7. Season with salt and cayenne. Reheat the puree in the microwave just before serving in 1-minute intervals, stirring occasionally.

Mashed Potatoes with Spinach

SERVES 8

TOTAL TIME: 40 MINUTES

Spinach and mashed potatoes— unexpected and fun!

   Coarse sea salt

4 Yukon Gold potatoes, peeled and cut into 1½-inch cubes

7 tablespoons extra-virgin olive oil, divided

6 tablespoons vegetable broth
   Freshly ground black pepper

1 (6-ounce) package baby spinach or fresh spinach

1 cup (packed) fresh basil leaves

1. Put potatoes in a large pot of salted water.

2. Bring to a boil and cook potatoes until tender, 15 to 20 minutes.

3. Drain potatoes and return to pot. Stir over low heat until excess moisture evaporates, 1 to 2 minutes.

4. Using a potato masher, mash warm potatoes.

5. Mix in the oil and broth and stir to blend.

6. Season to taste with coarse sea salt and freshly ground black pepper.

7. Heat 1 tablespoon oil in a heavy large skillet over medium-high heat.

8. Add spinach and toss 1 minute.

9. Add basil leaves and toss until wilted, 1 to 2 minutes longer.

10. Transfer mixture to a sieve set over a bowl. Drain well.

11. The potatoes and spinach can be made 2 hours ahead. Let stand separately at room temperature.

12. To finish, rewarm potatoes, adding more broth to moisten as needed. Stir in spinach mixture. Mound potatoes in a bowl and serve.

Vegetable Tart

SERVES 8

TOTAL TIME: 2 HOURS AND 15 MINUTES

I love to make tarts. They are always delicious with a simple salad. This one has lima beans, which I adore.

FOR THE PASTRY:

1½ cups whole wheat or all-purpose flour

½ cup fine cornmeal or polenta

1 teaspoon salt

2 tablespoons chopped chives

4 tablespoons cold Earth Balance "butter," cut into small pieces

4 tablespoons cold vegetable shortening

¼ cup plus 2 tablespoons ice water

FOR THE FILLING:

4 pounds lima beans, fresh or frozen

¾ pound thin asparagus, trimmed

3 tablespoons extra-virgin olive oil, plus more for brushing

10 large garlic cloves, thinly sliced

2 bunches scallions, thinly sliced

Sea salt and freshly ground black pepper

PASTRY:

1. In a food processor, combine the flour, cornmeal, salt, and chives, and process to blend.

2. Add the Earth Balance "butter" and pulse a few times until pea-size lumps form.

3. Add the shortening and pulse a few times.

4. Sprinkle the ice water over the mixture and pulse until the dough barely comes together.

5. Scrape the dough onto a lightly floured work surface and knead to form a ball.

6. Flatten the ball into a disk, wrap in plastic, and refrigerate for 1 hour, or until firm.

7. Preheat the oven to 400°F.

FILLING:

1. Fill a large skillet halfway with salted water and bring to a boil.

2. Add the limas and blanch.

3. Using a slotted spoon, transfer the limas to a baking sheet.

4. Add the asparagus to the boiling water and cook until tender, about 3 minutes.

5. Drain and transfer to a baking sheet to cool.

6. Cut the asparagus into 1-inch pieces.

7. Wipe out the skillet and heat 3 tablespoons olive oil.

8. Add the garlic and cook over low heat, stirring, until golden, 1½ minutes.

9. Add the scallions and cook over moderate heat until softened, 2 minutes.

10. Add the lima beans and asparagus and cook until heated through, 2 minutes.

11. Season with salt and pepper. Let cool.

THE TART:

1. On a floured work surface, roll out the pastry to a 14-inch round, about ⅛ inch thick.

2. Roll pastry around the rolling pin and carefully transfer to a parchment–paper–lined baking sheet.

3. Scrape the vegetable mixture into the center of the pastry, leaving a 1½-inch border all around.

4. Fold the edges up over the filling and brush the edges with olive oil.

5. Bake the tart on the bottom rack of the oven for about 30 minutes, until the crust is crisp on the bottom and golden brown.

6. Let the tart cool to warm.

7. Cut into wedges and serve.

Spaghetti Squash with Pine Nuts and Tarragon

SERVES 10

TOTAL TIME: 1 HOUR AND 30 MINUTES

You can do so much with spaghetti squash. It can be used like pasta. It's low in calories and very good for you!

½ cup pine nuts

3 large spaghetti squash halved lengthwise and seeded (9 pounds)

⅔ cup extra-virgin olive oil, plus more for drizzling

Sea salt and freshly ground black pepper

1 cup water

½ cup dry white wine

3 tablespoons white wine vinegar

1 teaspoon chopped thyme

Pinch of red pepper flakes

2 tablespoons chopped tarragon

1. Preheat the oven to 350°F.

2. Spread the pine nuts in a pie plate and bake for about 5 minutes, until golden brown. Transfer to a plate and let cool.

3. Arrange the spaghetti squash halves, cut-sides up on two rimmed baking sheets.

4. Drizzle with extra-virgin olive oil and season with salt and pepper.

5. Flip the squash, cut-sides down, and pour the water and wine into the pans.

6. Bake for 50 minutes, until the squash is just tender.

7. Flip the squash, cut-sides up, and let cool until warm.

8. Combine white wine vinegar with thyme and red pepper flakes in a small bowl.

9. Whisk in ⅔ cup olive oil and season with salt and pepper.

10. Using a fork, scrape out the spaghetti squash over a large bowl, separating the strands.

11. Pour the dressing over the squash and toss to coat.

12. Add the tarragon and pine nuts, and toss again.

13. Serve right away.

Polenta and Mushrooms

SERVES 4–6

ACTIVE TIME: 30 MINUTES

TOTAL TIME: 1 HOUR AND 20 MINUTES

A version of this recipe is the signature dish of one of my favorite chefs in New York City. It's comfort food with a twist!

FOR THE POLENTA:

- 6 cups water
- 2 cups coarse cornmeal or polenta
- 1 cup hemp milk
- 1 tablespoon Earth Balance "butter"
- ¼ cup nutritional yeast flakes
- 1 teaspoon sea salt (or to taste)
- 2 tablespoons minced fresh basil
- 2 tablespoons minced fresh thyme
  Freshly ground black pepper to taste

FOR THE MUSHROOMS:

- 2 tablespoons olive oil
- 1 small yellow onion, finely chopped
- 2 pounds assorted fresh mushrooms such as porcini, oyster, chanterelle, lobster, cremini, and shiitake, cleaned
- 4–5 tablespoons red wine, for deglazing
- 3–4 tablespoons balsamic vinegar
- 2 tablespoons Earth Balance "butter"
- 1 tablespoon minced fresh parsley, for garnish (optional)

TO MAKE THE POLENTA:

1. Heat the water to a boil.

2. Once the water has boiled, slowly add the cornmeal, and stir frequently over medium-low heat, careful not to let it boil over.

3. Slowly add milk and stir until the liquid is absorbed and the polenta thickens, about 30-40 minutes.

4. Remove from heat and add Earth Balance "butter" and herbs. Season with pepper. Set mixture aside for no more than 30 minutes while preparing mushrooms.

FOR THE MUSHROOMS:

1. In a large sauté pan, heat olive oil.

2. Add onion and cook for a few minutes until softened.

3. Add mushrooms and sauté over medium-high heat until mushrooms begin to go limp. Be careful not to overcook, or they will lose their flavor and become rubbery. Transfer to a plate or bowl.

4. Combine red wine and vinegar in same sauté pan.

5. Stir in Earth Balance "butter," add salt and pepper to taste, and remove from heat.

6. To serve, place a few spoonfuls of polenta in an individual bowl, top with mushrooms, and drizzle with wine sauce. Top with chopped parsley, if desired, and serve.

Three-Potato Roast

Serves 6

Total time: 1 hour

America's favorite vegetable, times 3.

1 pound red, white, or Yukon Gold potatoes, peeled and cut into ¾-inch cubes

1 (12-ounce) red-skinned sweet potato (yam), peeled and cut into ¾-inch cubes

1 (12-ounce) tan-skinned sweet potato, peeled and cut into ¾-inch cubes

¼ cup olive oil

1 tablespoon coarse sea salt

30 fresh medium sage leaves

1. Position a rack in center of oven; preheat to 425°F.

2. Combine all ingredients in a large bowl and toss to coat.

3. Spread mixture in a single layer on a large rimmed baking sheet.

4. Roast until potatoes are tender and browned around edges, stirring occasionally, about 40 minutes.

5. Serve roasted potatoes warm or at room temperature.

Tanya's Crumbly Apple Cobbler

Serves 8

Active time: 1 hour

Total time: 1 hour and 15 minutes

I begged my friend Tanya Petrovna, the chef and owner of Native Foods restaurants in California, for the recipe for her cobbler, which is one of the best things I have ever tasted.

7 Granny Smith apples
  Grated peel of 1 lemon

2 cups rolled oats

1½ cups unbleached flour

¼ teaspoon baking soda

1½ cups safflower oil

¾ cup maple syrup

1. Preheat oven to 425°F.

2. Peel, core, and slice apples in ¼-inch slices. Toss with lemon peel.

3. Arrange in a 9- by 14-inch baking pan.

4. Combine oats, flour, and baking soda well.

5. Mix in liquid ingredients to dry.

6. Spread oats and flour mixture over apples.

7. Bake, uncovered, for 15 minutes.

8. Cover with foil, reduce heat to 375°F, and let bake another 35 to 45 minutes until apples are soft.

9. Let cool and serve for dessert or breakfast.

Sweet Potato Pie

SERVES 8

ACTIVE TIME: 1 HOUR AND 10 MINUTES

TOTAL TIME: 1 HOUR AND 55 MINUTES

This is a nice change from pumpkin pie. There is something down-home about it that everyone loves.

CRUST:

- 1¼ cups whole wheat or all-purpose flour
- ¼ teaspoon salt
- ½ cup Earth Balance "butter," cut into small pieces
- 3 tablespoons ice water, or more if needed

FILLING:

- 2 cups sweet potatoes, peeled and diced
- 1 (12-ounce) package extra-firm silken tofu, drained and patted dry
- ¼ cup light brown sugar
    Prepared egg replacement mixture for 2 eggs
- ¼ cup pure maple syrup
- 1 tablespoon cornstarch
- 2 teaspoons ground cinnamon
- ½ teaspoon ground allspice
- ½ teaspoon ground ginger
- ½ teaspoon ground nutmeg

1. Preheat the oven to 400°F

2. Put washed potatoes on a baking sheet and bake for 45 minutes.

MAKE THE CRUST:

1. In a large bowl, combine the flour and salt.

2. Use a pastry blender to cut in the Earth Balance "butter" until the mixture looks like coarse crumbs.

3. Add the ice water a little at a time and blend until dough just starts to hold together.

4. Flatten the dough into a disk and wrap in plastic.

5. Refrigerate for 30 minutes while you prepare the filling.

MAKE THE FILLING:

1. In a food processor, combine the sweet potatoes and tofu until well blended.

2. Add the sugar, egg replacer, maple syrup, cornstarch, cinnamon, allspice, ginger, and nutmeg, mixing until smooth and well combined.

COMPLETE THE PIE:

1. Roll out dough on a lightly floured work surface to about 10 inches in diameter.

2. Fit the dough into a 9-inch pie plate and trim and crimp the edges.

3. Pour the filling into the crust and bake for 15 minutes.

4. Reduce the oven temperature to 350°F and bake for another 35 to 45 minutes, or until filling is set.

Pumpkin Bread Pudding

Serves 6

Active time: 10 minutes

Total time: 1 hour and 10 minutes

Bread pudding is one of the greatest nursery foods. It always reminds me of childhood. Pumpkins make this classic dessert perfect for fall.

 4 cups cubed whole grain bread

½ cup shelled pumpkin seeds (pepitas)

16 ounces fresh or canned pumpkin

¼ cup light brown sugar

 1 teaspoon pure vanilla extract

1½ teaspoons ground cinnamon

½ teaspoon ground allspice

½ teaspoon ground nutmeg

½ teaspoon salt

 2 cups plain or vanilla hemp milk

1. Preheat the oven to 350°F.

2. Grease a 9- by 13-inch baking pan.

3. Press half the bread cubes and half the pumpkin seeds into the bottom of the prepared baking pan and set aside.

4. In a large bowl, combine the pumpkin, sugar, vanilla, cinnamon, allspice, nutmeg, and salt.

5. Slowly whisk in the hemp milk until smooth and well combined.

6. Pour half of the pumpkin mixture over the bread in the pan, pushing the bread pieces down beneath the pumpkin mixture to moisten them.

7. Top with the remaining bread and pumpkin seeds, followed by the remaining pumpkin mixture.

8. Bake until firm, about 45 minutes.

9. Set aside for 15 minutes and serve, or refrigerate for 2 hours to serve chilled.

You can't live with them, and you can't live without them, but we make them taste good.

Mostly Greens

Dark green leafy vegetables have the most concentrated nutrition of any food. Though some people turn up their noses at greens, we should go out of our way to eat more. That is why I am doing a special section on greens. These are the vegetables we are talking about:

Arugula
Broccoli
Collard greens
Dandelion greens
Kale
Mustard greens
Romaine lettuce
Spinach
Swiss chard

They are a great source of vitamins A, C, folate (B_9), and K. Vitamin K has been getting a lot of attention lately. It has been found to protect bones from osteoporosis, reduce hardening of the arteries, regulate inflammation, and prevent diabetes. Greens contain iron, calcium, potassium, and magnesium as well as phytonutrients and omega-3 fats.

I've read that in prehistoric times, our ancestors ate six pounds of green leafy vegetables a day. Today, it's recommended that we eat only three cups of dark green vegetables a week, about a half cup each day. I've grouped some yummy green recipes in this special section to motivate you to add more greens to your diet. Once you try these recipes you will definitely want to eat more greens.

SOUPS

Chard Lentil Soup

SERVES 8
TOTAL TIME: 1 HOUR AND 20 MINUTES

This hearty soup is a meal in itself, a delicious main course. Serve with salad and some crusty bread and you have a satisfying meal for a chilly fall day or night.

1 cup dark mini-lentils such as Egyptian, Ethiopian, Spanish pardina, or Indian whole masoor dal
2 quarts vegetable stock
1 teaspoon sea salt
1 medium potato, peeled and sliced paper thin
1 onion, chopped
3 tablespoons olive oil
8 large Swiss chard leaves

1 pound leafy greens, such as spinach, dandelions, arugula, watercress, beet greens, kale, or a mixture

¼ cup roughly chopped fresh cilantro leaves

1 tablespoon minced garlic

⅓ cup freshly squeezed lemon juice

1. Wash and pick over the lentils.

2. Place lentils in a saucepan and cover with the stock or 2 quarts water with 1 teaspoon salt. Bring to a boil and skim off any foam that surfaces.

3. Add the potato, partially cover, and cook for 20 minutes.

4. In a large skillet, slowly brown the onion in the olive oil.

5. While onion is browning, wash, stem, and roughly shred the greens. You should have about 1 packed quart.

6. Add the cilantro and garlic to the skillet and sauté for a minute or two, then stir in the greens and allow them to wilt, covered.

7. Scrape the contents of the skillet, including the oil, into the saucepan and continue cooking another 20 minutes, or until thick and soupy.

8. Stir in the lemon juice and serve hot, lukewarm, or cool.

Potato Soup with Greens and Farro

Serves 6

Active time: 1 hour and 5 minutes

Total time: 13 hours and 5 minutes (overnight soak)

This flavorful soup works as a main course and it's good-looking, too. All you need is a delicious dark or crusty bread.

½ cup farro, picked over, rinsed, and soaked overnight in tepid water

3 tablespoons olive oil, plus more for garnish

½ cup chopped flat-leaf parsley

½ teaspoon red pepper flakes (without seeds), or more to taste

4 garlic cloves, peeled and sliced

½ pound boiling potatoes, peeled and chopped

¼ pound arugula leaves, stemmed and finely shredded

1 cup shelled peas

3 fresh asparagus spears, sliced very thin crosswise (optional)

Sea salt and freshly ground black pepper

3 cups vegetable stock

1. Drain the farro, cover with fresh cold water, and cook, covered, until tender, 45 minutes or longer.
2. In a heavy-bottomed bean or soup pot, heat the oil.
3. In another pot, bring vegetable stock to a simmer.
4. Add the parsley, red pepper flakes, garlic, and potatoes to the soup pot and sauté until soft and golden brown, about 15 minutes.
5. Mash the potatoes in the pot, so that they stick to the bottom of the pan and create caramelized areas here and there without burning.
6. Add the arugula, peas, and asparagus (if using), and stir-fry for a few minutes. Season with salt and pepper.
7. Add the fully cooked farro and 3 cups simmering stock and bring back to a boil. Cook at the simmer for 30 minutes to cook the vegetables and blend flavors.
8. Adjust the seasoning with salt and pepper.
9. Remove from the heat and let stand 5 minutes before serving.
10. Serve with a drizzle of fresh olive oil.

Kale with White Bean Sauté

SERVES 8

TOTAL TIME: 10 MINUTES

This is a classic Tuscan dish that is very nutritious. There's a reason why it's been around so long!

12	small to medium Tuscan kale leaves
2	tablespoons extra-virgin olive oil, plus more for garnish
1	garlic clove, peeled and thickly sliced
½	cup cooking liquid from the beans (if making from scratch) or use veggie broth
1½	cups white beans, cooked or canned
	Sea salt and freshly ground black pepper
3	cooked garlic cloves, peeled and halved

1. Remove the center rib from each leaf of kale. If leaves are long, tear each leaf into 4- or 5-inch lengths. Wash and pat dry.
2. In a 10-inch straight-sided skillet, heat 2 tablespoons olive oil.
3. Gradually add the leaves and cook, stirring, until they wilt and sizzle in the hot oil, 2 minutes.
4. Reduce the heat.
5. Add the sliced garlic, cover, and cook the leaves until tender, about 10 minutes.
6. Add liquid by the tablespoon, as needed, to keep the leaves from drying out.

7. Push the leaves to one side in the skillet; add the beans, salt and pepper, cooked garlic halves, and enough bean liquid to keep the dish juicy.

8. Cover and simmer for 5 minutes.

9. Serve warm with a drizzle of olive oil and freshly ground black pepper.

Braised Kale Spaghetti

SERVES 4

TOTAL TIME: 40 MINUTES WITH CANNED BEANS

This is a quick and easy main course. If you don't want to sauté the kale, you can steam it and toss it with the spaghetti separately.

- 1 pound lacinato kale, large center ribs and stems removed, cut crosswise into ½-inch slices (about 2 bunches)
- 3 tablespoons olive oil, divided
- 1 medium onion, finely chopped (about 1½ cups)
- 8 large garlic cloves, thinly sliced
- ½ pound spaghetti
- 2 teaspoons fresh lemon juice

1. Put on a medium-size pot of salted water to boil.

2. Rinse kale, drain, and transfer to a bowl.

3. Heat 1 tablespoon olive oil in large heavy pot over medium heat.

4. Add chopped onion and cook until translucent, 5 minutes.

5. Add garlic and cook until onions brown, 10 minutes.

6. Add kale, cover, and cook for 20 minutes. Steam kale until very wilted.

7. Cook spaghetti in a medium-size pot of boiling salted water until al dente, stirring occasionally.

8. Drain, reserving ¼ cup cooking liquid.

9. Add the cooked spaghetti to kale mixture in pot.

10. Add lemon juice and 2 tablespoons reserved cooking liquid by the tablespoonful if dry. Serve with a drizzle of olive oil.

11. If dry, finish with a drizzle of olive oil.

Greens and Mushroom Sauté

SERVES 10–12

TOTAL TIME: 30 MINUTES

Name a mushroom, and I'll love it. You can use any kind for this.

- 4 tablespoons extra-virgin olive oil, divided
- 1 pound any fresh mushrooms, stems trimmed, caps thinly sliced
  Coarse sea salt and freshly ground pepper
- ¾ cup vegetable broth, divided
- 1 bunch red Swiss chard, rinsed, stems cut from center of leaves, leaves cut into 1-inch-wide ribbons
- 1 bunch green Swiss chard, rinsed, stems cut from center of leaves, leaves cut into 1-inch-wide ribbons

1 head escarole, rinsed, leaves cut into 1-inch wide ribbons

2 cups chopped onions

4 garlic cloves, chopped

¼ teaspoon red pepper flakes

1. Heat 2 tablespoons oil in an extra-large skillet over high heat.

2. Add mushrooms; sprinkle with coarse salt and pepper.

3. Sauté until brown, about 10 minutes. Transfer to a bowl.

4. Pour ¼ cup broth into same skillet.

5. Add a third of the greens and sprinkle with coarse salt and pepper.

6. Toss until wilted but still bright green, about 2 minutes.

7. Transfer to a large strainer set over bowl.

8. Repeat 2 more times with remaining broth and greens. This portion of the recipe can be done 2 hours ahead. Let mushrooms and greens stand at room temperature and reserve skillet.

9. Heat 2 tablespoons oil in same skillet over medium-high heat.

10. Add onions. Sauté until beginning to color, about 5 minutes.

11. Add garlic and red pepper flakes and stir 1 minute.

12. Add greens and mushrooms. Toss to heat through, about 2 minutes. Season with salt and pepper.

13. Transfer to a bowl to serve.

Kale Chips

SERVES 4

TOTAL TIME: 40 MINUTES

Kale chips are everyone's favorite. This snack or side dish is irresistible.

1 pound curly kale, stems and large inner ribs removed

¼ cup extra-virgin olive oil

2 garlic cloves, minced

Sea salt and freshly ground black pepper

1. Preheat the oven to 375°F.

2. In a bowl, toss the kale with all but 1 tablespoon olive oil and half of the garlic.

3. Spread the kale on two baking sheets and roast in the upper and lower thirds of the oven for about 15 minutes, until crisp, switching the pan positions halfway through.

4. Season the kale with salt and pepper and transfer to a large platter to serve.

Mostly Beans

What I call beans are also known as legumes, and they include beans, peas, and lentils. Beans are a staple of a vegan or vegetarian diet. They are a good source of protein without the fat and cholesterol of meat. They are packed with important nutrients: magnesium, iron, potassium, and folate. Beans are also a source of soluble and insoluble fiber and good fats.

You can buy beans canned or in dried form. If you use canned beans, be sure to thoroughly rinse off the fluid the beans are packed in. You should rinse them several times. Most dry beans need to be soaked before cooking, so you have to build in time if you plan to use them. There are a few exceptions. **Dried lentils, split peas, and black-eyed peas do not need to be presoaked. It is important to soak all other dried beans.**

Dried beans have got to be soaked in water to rehydrate them. When you soak the beans, they will double in size, because they have absorbed the water. Soaking the beans breaks down the complex sugars that cause the gas and indigestion beans can cause. Those indigestible sugars dissolve into the water. That's why it is so important to rinse soaked beans a number of times. I find it easiest to soak them overnight, but there are several time-saving methods.

SPEED SOAK: If you are really pressed for time, you can add a pound of dried beans to a stockpot containing 10 cups of boiling water. Bring the water back to a boil, and boil the beans for 10 minutes. Then remove the pot from the heat, cover, and set aside for an hour. Rinse the beans thoroughly and cook as directed by the recipe.

FAST SOAK: If you have time to do the soak in the morning, bring 10 cups of water to a boil. Add 1 pound of dried beans and return to a boil. Remove from heat, cover, and set aside at room temperature for 2 or 3 hours. Rinse thoroughly.

SLOW SOAK: In a stockpot, cover 1 pound of dried beans with 10 cups of cold water. Cover and refrigerate for 6 to 8 hours or overnight. Rinse thoroughly, and you are ready to go.

SUPER SOAK: Put 1 pound of dried beans in a stockpot with at least 10 cups of boiling water. Boil for 3 minutes. Cover and set aside overnight. This method will dissolve most of the indigestible sugars. Make sure to rinse the beans several times after soaking to get rid of the troublemakers in the water.

The chart of cooking times that follows will help you select the beans you want to use.

COOKING CHART FOR BEANS

1 CUP BEANS	COOKING TIME
ADZUKI	50 minutes
BLACK BEANS	1–1½ hours
BLACK-EYED PEAS	45–60 minutes
CANNELLINI BEANS (WHITE KIDNEY)	1¼ hours
FAVA BEANS	1 hour
CHICKPEAS (GARBANZO BEANS)	1½ hours
GREAT NORTHERN BEANS	1 hour
KIDNEY BEANS, RED	1 hour
LENTILS, GREEN OR BROWN	35–40 minutes
LENTILS, RED	30 minutes
LIMA BEANS, BABY	40–45 minutes
LIMA BEANS, LARGE	1 hour
MUNG BEANS	45 minutes
NAVY BEANS	50–60 minutes
PEA BEANS	50–60 minutes
PEAS, SPLIT	50–60 minutes
PEAS, WHOLE	1¼ hours
PINTO BEANS	1 hour
SOYBEANS	3–4 hours

Pumpkin and Split Pea Soup

SERVES 12

TOTAL TIME: 30 MINUTES

Pumpkin—the perfect fall delight!

- 4 tablespoons Earth Balance "butter"
- 1 medium red onion, cut into ¼-inch dice
- 4 garlic cloves, minced
- 1 serrano chile, seeded and minced
- 1½ teaspoons ground cumin
- ½ teaspoon cayenne pepper
- 2 cups yellow split peas, soaked in water for 1 hour and drained
- 8½ cups water
- 1 (15-ounce) can unsweetened pumpkin puree
- ¾ pound fresh sugar pumpkin or butternut squash, peeled and cut into ¼-inch dice
- 1½ tablespoons fresh lemon juice
  Sea salt and freshly ground black pepper

1. In a large pot, melt the Earth Balance "butter."
2. Add the onion, garlic, and chile and cook over moderately high heat until the onion is softened, 4 minutes.
3. Add the cumin and cayenne and cook until fragrant, about 1 minute.
4. Add the split peas and water.
5. Whisk in the pumpkin puree and bring to a simmer.
6. Cover and cook over moderately low heat, stirring occasionally, until the split peas are tender.
7. Stir in lemon juice. Add salt and freshly ground pepper to taste.

White Bean and Escarole Soup. My father gave me the two dogs for Christmas so they are always on the table Christmas Eve.

White Bean and Escarole Soup

SERVES 8

TOTAL TIME: 1 HOUR WITH CANNED
BEANS; 2 HOURS WITH DRIED BEANS

Another classic, escarole and beans.

¾ cup dried white beans or 1½ cups canned
   white beans (Great Northern or cannellini)

4 cups cold water

1 tablespoon olive oil

2 medium onions, diced

5 garlic cloves, thinly sliced

4 celery stalks, plus hearts, diced

1 teaspoon dried basil

½ teaspoon dried thyme

2 medium bay leaves

6 cups vegetable stock

1 (24-ounce) can diced tomatoes with juice

1 teaspoon sea salt

¼ teaspoon black pepper

1 pound escarole, cleaned, trimmed, and
   chopped

½ cup chopped fresh basil

1. Wash the dried beans in a large colander, checking very carefully for stones.
2. Place the beans in a 2-quart pot and cover with 4 cups cold water.
3. Place over high heat and bring to a boil.
4. Reduce the heat and simmer until the beans are soft, about 40 minutes, skimming off any foam. The cooked beans should be covered by a scant inch of cooking liquid when done. Add more water as necessary.
5. Reserve the beans in the cooking liquid.
6. If using canned beans, rinse in a colander.
7. Heat the oil in a soup pot over medium-high heat and sauté the onions, garlic, celery, and dried herbs until the vegetables begin to soften.
8. Add the stock to the pot, raise the heat to high, and bring the soup to a boil, 20 minutes.
9. Add the beans and their cooking liquid, tomatoes and their juice, salt, and pepper and mix well. Taste and adjust the seasonings. Warm the soup over medium heat.
10. Remove and discard bay leaves.
11. Just before serving, add the escarole and cook for 4 minutes, or until the escarole is tender.
12. Add the fresh basil.

Curry Chickpea Soup

SERVES 6
TOTAL TIME: 30 MINUTES

Curry and chickpeas. Yum, yum, yum!

2 (19-ounce) cans chickpeas, drained
1 (13½-ounce) can light coconut milk
1 (14½-ounce) can whole tomatoes, or ½ cup fresh, drained and chopped
¼ cup cilantro leaves
½ teaspoon garam masala (an Indian blend of spices)
½ teaspoon ground ginger
1 cup vegetable broth
  Sea salt and freshly ground black pepper
2 scallions, green parts only, thinly sliced

1. In a blender, combine the drained chickpeas with the coconut milk, chopped tomatoes, cilantro leaves, garam masala, and ground ginger, and puree until smooth.
2. Transfer the puree to a medium saucepan. Stir in the vegetable broth and bring to a simmer over moderately high heat.
3. Season with salt and pepper.
4. Ladle the soup into bowls, top with scallion greens, and serve.

Special Bean Dishes

White Beans

Serves 6
Active time: 1 hour and 15 minutes
Total time: 10 hours and 15 minutes
(overnight soak)

This is a classic bean recipe that makes a perfect side dish.

 1   cup dried white beans
4-5 garlic cloves, unpeeled
     Aromatics tied in cheesecloth:
 1   sprig thyme
 2   onion slices
 1   carrot
 2   small sprigs celery
 3   sprigs parsley
 1   bay leaf
12   peppercorns
½   teaspoon salt

1. Pick over and rinse the beans. Cover with water and soak overnight.
2. Drain beans; place in a deep clay pot with the garlic, and cover with at least 3 inches of water.
3. Bring to a boil, carefully skimming foam.
4. Add the bag of aromatics, pushing it into beans.
5. Simmer, partially, covered for 30 minutes, then add salt and simmer 10 to 20 minutes

more, until the beans are tender. (The time needed will vary, depending on the age of the beans. To test whether beans are almost done, remove 1 or 2 beans with a spoon and blow gently on them. If they are close to ready, the skin will burst.)
6. Simmer another 2 to 3 minutes, then remove from the heat, Allow beans to cool in the cooking liquid. Discard aromatics but not the garlic.

Chickpea Fries

Serves 4
Active time: 20 minutes
Total time: 6 hours and 20 minutes
(cooling time)

These are delicious!

 2   cups chickpea flour
 2   tablespoons minced parsley
 1   garlic clove, minced
 ½   teaspoon freshly ground black pepper
     Sea salt
2⅓ cups water
     Canola or grapeseed oil, for frying

1. In a heavy medium saucepan, combine the chickpea flour with the parsley, garlic, pepper, and 1 teaspoon salt.
2. Whisk in the water in a thin stream until a smooth paste forms. Heat the mixture over moderately high heat, whisking constantly, until very thick, about 5 minutes.

3. Beat with a wooden spoon until smooth.

4. Scrape the dough into a 12- by 7½-inch baking dish and smooth the surface.

5. Let cool to room temperature. Press a piece of plastic wrap directly on the dough and refrigerate for at least 6 hours or overnight.

6. In a medium skillet, heat 2 inches of oil to 350°F.

7. Unmold the chickpea dough onto a cutting board.

8. Cut it in half lengthwise, then slice crosswise into ½-inch-wide sticks.

9. Fry the chickpea sticks in 2 batches until golden brown, 2 to 3 minutes.

10. Using a slotted spoon, transfer the fries to paper towels to drain. Sprinkle with salt and serve at once.

Lentils with Red Wine

SERVES 4

TOTAL TIME: 1 HOUR AND 15 MINUTES

With this you don't need anything else— maybe just a delicious piece of bread.

1½ cups (12 ounces) French green lentils
    Sea salt
 1 tablespoon extra-virgin olive oil
 1 small red onion, finely chopped
 1 garlic clove, minced
¼ cup dry red wine
 1 packed cup baby spinach (2 ounces)
½ cup vegetable stock
 4 cups lightly packed mâche or arugula (2 ounces)
¼ cup chopped flat-leaf parsley
¼ cup chopped cilantro
    Freshly ground black pepper

1. In a large saucepan, cover the lentils with 2 inches of water and bring to a boil. Season with salt and simmer over moderate heat until tender, 40 minutes.

2. Drain the lentils.

3. Heat the olive oil in a large, deep skillet.

4. Add the red onion and cook over moderate heat, stirring occasionally, until softened, about 5 minutes.

5. Add the garlic and cook until fragrant, about 1 minute.

6. Add the lentils and wine and simmer until the wine has been absorbed, about 5 minutes.

7. Add the spinach and stock and cook, stirring occasionally, until the spinach is wilted, about 5 minutes.

8. Add the mâche or arugula, parsley, and cilantro, and cook until barely wilted, about 2 minutes.

9. Season with salt and pepper and serve warm.

PART 5

WINTER

A cozy dinner by the fire, Shepherd's Pie,
Flourless Chocolate Tart, and some good red wine.

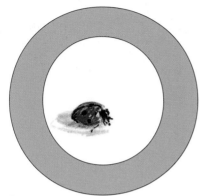ne of my favorite times in Mother Nature is after a big snowstorm. The stillness and silence—everything is asleep, tucked away nice and warm under the snow. All my dogs and I love to go out and play, and then we all come in to warm up in front of a big fire.

I always make sure my bird feeders are full during the winter months, and enjoy watching the pecking order of chickadees, sparrows, blue jays, woodpeckers, nuthatches, cardinals, tufted titmice, and juncos as they help themselves. On Christmas Day, I make a huge batch of nuts and seeds and put them all over the place for all the critters that live at Templeton. Every year I make a gingerbread house that I put out for the squirrels. I make sure everyone has a fat tummy at Christmas.

Soups and stews on the stove and chestnuts roasting away in the oven make the house smell delicious. It is a season for full-bodied red wine and brandy, brunches, and early Sunday dinners with friends. It is also a season of presents and pull-out-all-the-stops holiday parties. Christmas Eve is always black tie, but the formality stops there!

When days are short, curling up with a book in a bed made with flannel sheets and a fluffy down comforter is de rigueur, and my dogs are the best hot water bottles ever. A window is always open in my room regardless

Cornelia Guest Cookies on an old chair. The tapestry is an Aesop Fable, they were my favorites as a child.

of the temperature outside so that the tip of my nose stays cold. It makes going to sleep more delicious and gives me rosy cheeks. Nature, too, needs time to restore herself and to prepare for the growth of spring.

It gets dark early in the winter, so I like to light a fire, grab a glass of red wine, and cook. What I want to eat in the winter is so different from the light foods of summer and spring. We all need robust food that keeps us warm and fills us up. I like dinners in front of the fire when the days are short and cold.

When we plant bulbs in pots—paperwhites are my favorites—Thanksgiving and Christmas are around the corner. We also plant seeds indoors so that the seedlings are ready to go out when the ground thaws in the spring.

WINTER FLOWERS Amaryllis (indoors) • Crocus • Cyclamen Helleborus • Holly berries • Mistletoe Scilla • Snowdrop • Winter jasmine Witch hazel

One of the things I relish most about winter is the pluck of its blooms. What moxie the camellia japonica possesses! There's nothing more simple or elegant than camellia blooms floating in a silver or pewter Revere bowl by candlelight. Lenten roses defy the elements in winter and are lovely floating in a nut dish or bud vase.

One of my all-time favorite winter tricks is to find lichen-covered branches in my yard and place them in an old urn. Just walk around and see what you come up with! If you are a city mouse, branches can be had at your neighborhood flower shop.

MARGOT SHAW
Editor, Flower *magazine*

The painting of my father, Winston, with his grandmother, Annie Phipps.

COZY WINTER SUPPER

This is one of my favorite dinners for those cold winter nights.

MENU

Shepherd's Pie

Flourless Chocolate Tart

Chocolate Mousse Balls

Shepherd's Pie

Serves 4

Total time: 2 hours

This is one of my all-time favorite dinners. When I was little, we had it all the time. It takes a bit of work, so I make a few and freeze them.

- 2 pounds potatoes (I use Yukon Gold)
- 1 large onion
- 2 large carrots
- 2 celery stalks
- 1 pound favorite mushrooms
- ¼ cup plus 2 tablespoons olive oil, divided
- 2 leeks, cut into 1-inch pieces
  Sea salt and freshly ground pepper
- 1 cup canned or fresh vegetable stock
- 2 pounds cubed seitan
- 2 (14½-ounce) cans diced tomatoes
- 1 (10-ounce) box frozen peas
  or 1½ cups fresh peas, cooked

1. Preheat oven to 325°F.

2. Peel potatoes and cover with water. Bring to a boil and cook until ready for mashing, approximately 30 minutes.

3. Coarsely dice onion, carrots, and celery separately.

4. Remove stems from mushrooms.

5. If you are making your own stock, take the onion, carrot, and celery trimmings and mushroom stems, add a quart of water, bring to a boil, and simmer down to a cup, approximately 45 minutes. Strain before using.

6. Lay mushrooms and carrots on a baking sheet, sprinkle with olive oil, salt and pepper, and roast for 45 minutes.

7. Lay onion, celery, and leeks on another baking sheet and sprinkle with olive oil, salt, and pepper. Roast for 20 to 30 minutes or until tender.

8. Drain the potatoes after 30 minutes or when they are fork-tender. Reserve a cup of the water the spuds were cooked in.

9. Mash the potatoes and add ¼ cup olive oil, a teaspoon each of salt and pepper, and the reserved water.

10. Combine the stock, seitan, and diced tomatoes in a 4 quart saucepot and let simmer for 45 minutes.

11. Add the cooked peas and roasted vegetables during the last 5 minutes.

12. Transfer to a 10- by 14-inch casserole dish and cover with a 1½-inch layer of mashed potatoes.

13. Roast in the top rack of the oven for 20 to 25 minutes.

14. Put the casserole under the broiler for a few minutes to brown.

Flourless Chocolate Tart

SERVES 6
ACTIVE TIME: 30 MINUTES
TOTAL TIME: 2 HOURS AND 30 MINUTES

There are a few things I can't live without, and chocolate is one of them!

16 ounces nondairy semisweet or dark chocolate chips
1 cup raw pecans
1 cup raw walnuts
¼ cup cane sugar
4 tablespoons Earth Balance "butter"
2 cups nondairy milk
2 tablespoons cornstarch powder
¼ cup water

1. Preheat oven to 375°F.
2. Melt the chocolate in a double boiler or microwave.
3. Pulverize pecans, walnuts, and sugar in a food processor.
4. Add Earth Balance "butter" and process until a thick batter forms.
5. Press batter into a 9- or 10-inch tart pan.
6. Bake the crust for 10 minutes, or until golden brown. Remove from oven and place on a rack to cool.
7. In a saucepan, heat milk over medium heat. It should be scalding hot but not boiling.
8. While milk is heating, combine cornstarch and water in a bowl or measuring cup until powder completely dissolves. This is your thickener.
9. Add melted chocolate to milk, and whisk to combine thoroughly.
10. Whisk in thickener and stir well.
11. Lower heat and simmer for 10 minutes, stirring occasionally. The chocolate mixture will thicken.
12. Pour mixture into the baked tart shell and chill for at least 2 hours or as long as overnight.

Chocolate Mousse Balls

SERVES 4
TOTAL TIME: UNDER 15 MINUTES

When I need a chocolate fix, this is what I make. It's quick and satisfies that craving.

5 ounces vegan chocolate
5 pitted dates
1 teaspoon agave or maple syrup or more if you really like sweets
¼ cup shredded coconut
1 tablespoon cacao powder

1. Melt the chocolate in a double boiler.
2. Put chocolate, dates, and sweetener in a food processor and blend.
3. Use a melon scoop to take out some of the mixture and shape it into a ball with your hands.
4. Roll the ball in coconut or cacao, and repeat with the rest of the mixture.

There are fewer vegetables and fruits in the winter, but Mother Nature knows what she's doing. The vegetables are heavier and heartier to keep us warm and get us through the cold days, and the fruits are brighter.

WINTER VEGETABLES

Beets • Belgian endives • Broccoli • Brussels sprouts • Collard greens
Carrots • Cauliflower • Daikon radish • Kale • Mushrooms • Onions
Rutabaga • Sweet potatoes • Turnips • Winter squash

WINTER FRUITS

Apples • Grapefruit • Oranges • Papayas • Pomegranates • Tangerines

WINTER DRINK

Hot Chocolate Tea

SERVES 2

My father had tea every day at five. And since I love chocolate, I thought this was a great way to combine the two. It brings back wonderful memories of many teatimes spent with my father on cold, snowy days.

6 tablespoons Dutch process cacao powder

¼ cup agave

2 tablespoons loose-leaf premium Earl Grey tea

2 cups boiling water

Place cacao and agave in a heatproof pitcher. Place tea in a second pitcher or bowl and pour 2 cups boiling water over it. Steep for about 3 minutes. Strain over cacao and agave. Whisk until slightly frothy. Serve in two cups.

Hot Chocolate Tea with Cornelia Guest Cookies, surrounded by family pictures.

*Artichoke and White Bean Puree.
Maze in the picture with her favorite cat
Minou! She was everything to me. I love
everything animal related, hence the
painting, napkins, and sculpture.*

Artichoke and White Bean Puree

SERVES 6
TOTAL TIME: 5 MINUTES

This is very creamy and quick to whip up.

- 1 (6-ounce) jar marinated artichoke hearts, drained
- 1½ cups cooked or 1 (15½-ounce) can white beans, drained and rinsed
- 1 tablespoon chopped fresh parsley
- 1 tablespoon olive oil
- 2 tablespoons fresh lemon juice
- ½ teaspoon salt
- ¼ teaspoon ground cayenne pepper

1. In a food processor, combine the artichoke hearts, beans, parsley, oil, lemon juice, salt, and cayenne. Process until well blended.
2. Taste, adjusting seasonings if necessary.
3. Transfer to a medium-size bowl and serve. If not using right away, cover and refrigerate until needed.

Black Bean Hummus

SERVES 6
TOTAL TIME: UNDER 15 MINUTES

Hummus is nutritious, delicious, and easy to make!

- ½ cup chopped fresh cilantro, divided
- 2 tablespoons tahini
- 2 tablespoons water
- 2 tablespoons fresh lime juice
- 1 tablespoon extra-virgin olive oil
- ¾ teaspoon ground cumin
- ¼ teaspoon sea salt
- 1 (15-ounce) can black beans, rinsed and drained
- 1 garlic clove, peeled
- 3 (6-inch) pitas or raw vegetable crudités

1. Preheat oven to 425°F
2. Put ¼ cup cilantro, tahini, water, lime juice, olive oil, cumin, salt, beans, and garlic in a food processor and process until smooth.
3. Spoon into a bowl; sprinkle with remaining ¼ cup cilantro.
4. Cut each pita into 8 wedges.
5. Arrange on a baking sheet. Bake for 6 minutes, turning once. Or serve hummus with raw vegetable crudités.

Winter Soups

Nothing's better than hot soup in the winter, so I am giving you a bunch of my favorites.

Cream of Mushroom Soup

SERVES 4

TOTAL TIME: 45 MINUTES

I love mushrooms and the coconut adds flavor. The best thing about this recipe... it's so easy to make!

- 2 tablespoons Earth Balance "butter"
- 8 ounces button mushrooms, sliced
- 8 ounces portobello mushroom caps, sliced
- 2 tablespoons minced garlic
- 2 (14-ounce) cans coconut milk
  Sea salt and pepper to taste
  Shredded coconut, for garnish

1. Melt Earth Balance "butter" in a pan and sauté mushrooms and garlic for 7 to 10 minutes, or until mushrooms have shrunk in size by about half.
2. Add coconut milk and bring to a boil.
3. Reduce heat and simmer for 15 minutes.
4. Using an immersion or countertop blender, puree until smooth.
5. Season with salt and pepper and garnish with the shredded coconut.

Squash Soup with Pumpkin Seeds

SERVES 10–12

TOTAL TIME: 1 HOUR AND 15 MINUTES

I think winter squash is delicious. I love crunchy pumpkin seeds sprinkled on top.

- 4 tablespoons Earth Balance "butter"
- 1 medium onion, coarsely chopped
- 1 celery stalk, coarsely chopped
- 2 garlic cloves, coarsely chopped
- 1 cup dry white wine
- 1 quart vegetable stock
- 1 quart water
- 4 pounds kabocha or butternut squash, peeled, seeded, and cut into 1-inch cubes
  Sea salt and freshly ground white pepper
  Large pinch of freshly grated nutmeg
  Salted roasted pumpkin seeds

1. In a large pot, melt the Earth Balance "butter." Add the onion, celery, and garlic, and cook over moderate heat, stirring, until softened, about 5 minutes. Add the white wine and simmer for 3 minutes. Add the stock and water and bring to a boil. Add the squash, cover partially, and simmer over moderately low heat until tender, about 30 minutes.
2. Working in batches, puree the soup in a blender. Return the soup to the pot, bring to a simmer, and season with salt, white pepper, and nutmeg. Garnish with pumpkin seeds.

Broccoli Soup

*Broccoli soup is a favorite of mine.
It's always a fun, different starter.*

- 1 tablespoon olive oil
- 1 medium onion, chopped
- ⅛ teaspoon red pepper flakes (optional)
- 2 cups vegetable broth
- 1 bunch broccoli, florets coarsely chopped and stems peeled and sliced (about 7 cups)
- 1 large russet potato, peeled and cut into ½-inch pieces
- 2 cups water
- ½ teaspoon sea salt
- ¼ teaspoon freshly ground black pepper

1. Heat oil in a large saucepan over medium heat.

2. Add the onion and red pepper flakes (if using) and cook, stirring occasionally, until the onion is soft, 4 to 6 minutes.

3. Add the broth, broccoli, potato, 2 cups water, salt, and black pepper to the saucepan, and bring to a boil.

4. Reduce heat and simmer, covered, until the vegetables are very tender, 18 to 20 minutes.

5. In a blender, working in batches, puree the soup until smooth, adjusting the consistency with water as necessary; or use a handheld immersion blender in the saucepan. Serve immediately.

Winter Vegetable Soup

SERVES 8
ACTIVE TIME: 20 MINUTES
TOTAL TIME: 1 HOUR AND 15 MINUTES

This soup is pure winter—full of root vegetables with just a little green, like the pine trees in the snow. I serve it for lunch with hummus and crusty bread. And afterwards... a nice nap!

- 2 tablespoons extra-virgin olive oil
- 1 medium carrot, sliced
- 2 leeks, white and tender green parts only, thinly sliced
- 1 stalk celery, chopped
- 1 large onion, thinly sliced
- 2 turnips, chopped
- 2 garlic cloves, minced
- 1 cup pearl barley
- 8 cups vegetable broth
- 4 cups water
- 10 sprigs thyme
- 2 bay leaves
- 1½ pounds celery root, peeled and cut into ½-inch cubes
- 1 pound parsnips, peeled and cut into ½-inch pieces
  Sea salt and freshly ground black pepper
- 1 pound baby spinach
- 1 teaspoon freshly grated nutmeg

1. Heat the oil in a large pot.

2. Add the carrots, leek, celery, onion, turnip, and garlic and cook over moderate

Winter Vegetable Soup. It's so filling you don't need much else.

heat, stirring occasionally, until tender, about 5 minutes.

3. Stir in the barley.

4. Add the vegetable broth, water, thyme, and bay leaves, and bring to a boil.

5. Add the celery root and parsnips and season with salt and pepper.

6. Simmer over moderately low heat until the barley and root vegetables are tender, about 40 minutes.

7. Add spinach and nutmeg, and stir until spinach is limp, about 3 minutes.

Kale and Cabbage Soup

Serves 6

Active time: 20 minutes

Total time: 1 hour and 30 minutes

This rustic soup is a classic. Serve it with hot, coarse peasant bread.

1   tablespoon extra-virgin olive oil

1   medium onion, finely diced

2   garlic cloves, minced

1¼ cups farro

½ head Savoy cabbage, tough stems
  discarded, leaves torn into large pieces
½ bunch red Russian kale, stems discarded
2 quarts vegetable broth
1 cup water
6 sprigs thyme
1 small sprig rosemary
  Sea salt and freshly ground black pepper
½ cup finely chopped flat-leaf parsley

1. Preheat oven to 350°F.
2. Heat the oil in an enameled cast-iron casserole.
3. Add the onion and garlic and cook until softened, 5 minutes.
4. Add the farro and cook, stirring, for 3 minutes.
5. Add the cabbage and kale and cook, stirring, until just wilted.
6. Add the vegetable broth, water, thyme, and rosemary, and bring to a simmer.
7. Cover the soup, transfer to the oven, and cook for about 1 hour, until the farro and greens are tender. Alternatively, simmer the soup over moderate heat for 1 hour.
8. Season the soup with salt and pepper.
9. Transfer the soup to a tureen, sprinkle with parsley, and serve.

Vegetable Broth

SERVES 8
TOTAL TIME: 3 HOURS

This is a perfect light broth to start any meal. Vegetable broth is the base for so many recipes that you should always have some in the freezer. You can freeze the broth in 1-cup containers or in frozen cubes from an ice cube tray to cook with later. This recipe makes 8 cups. You'll see that homemade broth tastes so much better, is not that difficult to make, and is so worth it.

2 tablespoons extra-virgin olive oil
4 medium carrots, cut into 3-inch lengths
3 large leeks, white parts chopped, green tops reserved and coarsely chopped
3 large celery stalks, cut into 3-inch lengths, leaves reserved
2 large onions, peeled and quartered
1 small turnip, peeled and quartered
3 large garlic cloves, peeled and halved
10 cups water
1 cup coarsely chopped fresh parsley, stems included
¼ cup coarsely chopped sprigs thyme, stems included
1 large bay leaf
¼ teaspoon whole black peppercorns
¼ teaspoon whole allspice
  Sea salt and freshly ground black pepper to taste

1. In a large stockpot, heat the oil over medium-low heat. Add the carrots, leeks, celery, onions, turnip, and garlic.
2. Cook, covered, stirring occasionally, until vegetables are soft, about 45 minutes.
3. Uncover and increase heat to medium. Cook, stirring occasionally, about 15 minutes, or until vegetables are light golden brown and brown bits are forming at the bottom of the pot.
4. Add water and remaining ingredients, including the reserved leek tops and reserved celery leaves.
5. Bring to a boil over high heat, scraping the bottom to release the browned bits.
6. Reduce the heat and simmer gently, uncovered, 1½ hours, stirring occasionally.
7. Strain the stock into a bowl through a sieve or colander, pressing firmly on the solids to extract as much of the liquid as possible, then discard the vegetables.
8. Season with salt and pepper.

Spinach Tofu Lasagna

SERVES 8
ACTIVE TIME: 30 MINUTES
TOTAL TIME: 1 HOUR AND 15 MINUTES

Who can live without lasagna? You don't have to give it up when you are not eating animal products. This will fill the bill.

½ to 1 pound whole wheat lasagna noodles
2 (10-ounce) packages frozen chopped spinach, thawed and drained, or 20 ounces fresh spinach, blanched
1 (16-ounce) package firm tofu (not silken)
¼ cup hemp milk
2 garlic cloves, peeled
1 tablespoon lemon juice
2 tablespoons minced fresh basil (about 20 leaves)
1 tablespoon sea salt (or to taste)
4–6 cups tomato or pasta sauce of your choice

1. Preheat oven to 350°F.
2. Cook lasagna noodles according to package directions, or use fresh lasagna noodles and cook until tender. Drain and set aside.
3. Squeeze as much water from spinach as possible and set aside. If using fresh spinach, blanch first, dropping spinach into boiling water and leaving for 2 minutes before draining.

4. Place tofu, milk, garlic, lemon juice, basil, and salt in a blender or food processor, and blend until smooth. You have just made tofu "ricotta." It should be creamy but still have body.

5. Transfer to a large bowl and stir in spinach.

6. Season with salt to taste.

7. Cover bottom of a 9- by 13-inch baking dish with a thin layer of tomato sauce, then a layer of noodles (use about one third of noodles). Follow with half the tofu filling.

8. Continue in the same order, using half the remaining tomato sauce and noodles, and all remaining tofu filling. End with remaining noodles, covered by remaining tomato sauce. Bake for 40 to 45 minutes, until hot and bubbling.

Penne with Potatoes and Chard

SERVES 6
TOTAL TIME: 50 MINUTES

Potatoes and pasta? Sounds like heaven, especially in the winter.

1	pound new potatoes, diced
4	tablespoons olive oil
1	pound whole wheat penne
1	onion, chopped
1	pound chard, leaves removed from stems

1. Preheat the oven to 425°F.

2. Toss potatoes and 2 tablespoons olive oil in a roasting pan.

3. Roast, stirring occasionally, until browned and very tender, about 30 minutes.

4. Cook penne according to package directions.

5. Meanwhile, cook the onion in the remaining 2 tablespoons olive oil over medium heat, stirring, for 5 minutes.

6. Add the chard stems and cook until they soften, a minute or two.

7. Add the chard leaves, cover, and cook until tender, about 5 minutes.

8. Toss chard with potatoes and whole wheat penne and serve.

Penne with Peas and Mushrooms

SERVES 4
TOTAL TIME: 30 MINUTES

Peas are great protein. Add wild mushrooms and you have the most delicious pasta.

2	tablespoons extra-virgin olive oil
1	small onion, chopped
½	pound fresh wild or cremini mushrooms, thinly sliced
1	pound diced tomatoes
1	cup frozen green peas or 1½ cups fresh peas
	Sea salt and freshly ground black pepper, to taste

Penne with Peas and Mushrooms. A classic! My father loved birds. These were his favorite plates and he liked having dinners served in them.

Crushed red pepper flakes to taste

8   ounces penne

1   tablespoon parsley

1. Put a large pot of salted water on to boil.

2. In a large deep-sided nonstick skillet, heat the oil over medium heat.

3. Add the onion and cook, stirring, until softened, 3 to 4 minutes.

4. Add the mushrooms and cook, stirring, 1 minute.

5. Add the tomatoes and their juices, peas, salt, black pepper, and red pepper flakes. Bring to brisk simmer over medium-high heat. Reduce the heat and simmer gently, stirring occasionally until the mixture thickens, about 10 minutes.

6. Cook penne in boiling water for 12 minutes, then drain.

7. Add the pasta and parsley and thoroughly combine.

8. Serve right away.

French Onion Tart

SERVES 10
ACTIVE TIME: 45 MINUTES
TOTAL TIME: 1 HOUR AND 30 MINUTES

This tart can be a casual main course, or a first course at a more formal dinner. It always works.

2 uncooked pie shells, thawed (If you are feeling ambitious, you can make your own from scratch from the All-Purpose Piecrust recipe on page 86.)
5 large yellow or white onions, thinly sliced
4 garlic cloves, minced
1 tablespoon Earth Balance "butter"
½ teaspoon salt, plus a little extra
1½ cups hemp milk
15 ounces extra-firm tofu (not silken)
½ teaspoon freshly ground black pepper
½ teaspoon nutmeg
5 tablespoons whole wheat flour
2 tablespoons nutritional yeast flakes (optional)

1. Preheat oven to 350°F.
2. Bake pie shells for 10 minutes and remove from oven. Set aside.
3. In a large sauté pan, cook onions and garlic in Earth Balance "butter," stirring occasionally, until onions become translucent, 4 to 6 minutes. Add salt to taste.
Cook for 15 to 25 minutes longer to caramelize the onions.
4. In a blender or large food processor, combine milk, tofu, remaining ½ teaspoon salt, pepper, nutmeg, flour, and nutritional yeast (if using) until mixture is smooth.
5. In a large bowl, add the contents of the blender to the sautéed onions. Stir all ingredients together.
6. Distribute evenly between the 2 partially cooked pie shells.
7. Bake for 45 minutes, or until crust is golden brown and filling sets.
8. Serve immediately.

Roast Potatoes with Truffle Oil

SERVES 8
TOTAL TIME: 45 MINUTES

How can you go wrong with truffle oil?

1½ pounds red potatoes, cut into wedges
2 tablespoons olive oil
1 tablespoon minced garlic
½ teaspoon sea salt
½ teaspoon freshly ground black pepper
1 tablespoon white truffle oil
2 teaspoons fresh thyme leaves

1. Preheat oven to 450°F.
2. Place potatoes in a roasting pan.
3. Drizzle potatoes with olive oil and sprinkle with garlic, salt, and pepper. Toss well to combine.

French Onion Tart. This is delicious anytime! Lunch, dinner, leftovers.

4. Bake for 35 minutes or until potatoes are browned and tender.

5. Remove from the oven and drizzle potatoes with truffle oil and sprinkle with thyme. Toss gently to combine.

Spicy Roast Broccoli

SERVES 4
TOTAL TIME: 18 MINUTES

It's always fun to serve familiar food in a new way.

6 cups broccoli florets

2 tablespoons dark sesame oil

2 teaspoons sambal oelek (ground fresh chile paste) or other chile paste

⅜ teaspoon salt

6 large garlic cloves, coarsely chopped

1. Place a small roasting pan in oven and preheat oven to 450°F.

2. Place broccoli in a large bowl; drizzle with oil. Toss to coat.

3. Add sambal oelek and salt to broccoli mixture and toss.

4. Transfer broccoli mixture to hot roasting pan.
5. Bake for 5 minutes.
6. Remove from the oven, add garlic to the pan, and stir.
7. Bake an additional 5 minutes, or until broccoli is lightly browned.

Gingered Winter Squash

SERVES 4
TOTAL TIME: 1 HOUR AND 15 MINUTES

Squash with a kick!

- ½ cup water
- ½ cup red wine vinegar
- 1 cinnamon stick
- 2½ pounds thick-fleshed sugar pumpkin or acorn squash, halved and seeded
- 1 tablespoon olive oil
- Coarse sea salt and freshly ground black pepper
- 1 (1-inch) piece fresh ginger, peeled

1. Preheat the oven to 325°F.
2. In a small saucepan, combine the water with the vinegar and cinnamon and simmer for 5 minutes, stirring. Remove from heat.
3. While the liquid is simmering, line a baking sheet with aluminum foil.
4. Rub the squash with olive oil and season with salt and pepper.

5. Using a fine grater, grate the ginger over the cut sides of the squash and rub it into the flesh.
6. Transfer the squash to the prepared baking sheet, cut-side down, and roast for about 15 minutes, until the squash starts to soften.
7. Turn the squash, cut-side up and roast for about 17 minutes longer, until tender.
8. Transfer to a work surface and let cool slightly.
9. Increase the oven temperature to 425°F.
10. Cut the squash into 1½-inch-thick wedges.
11. Lightly rub the foil with oil.
12. Arrange the squash on a baking sheet and roast for about 25 minutes, turning once halfway through, until golden and crisp along the edges.
13. Arrange the squash on a platter. Discard the cinnamon stick and drizzle the liquid over the squash.

Roast Cabbage and Brussels Sprouts

SERVES 4
TOTAL TIME: 40 MINUTES

This is a simple, fun way to eat your veggies in the winter.

- ½ cup pine nuts
- 1 pound brussels sprouts, quartered
- 6 tablespoons olive oil

Sea salt and freshly ground black pepper

1 teaspoon Dijon mustard

⅛ teaspoon cayenne pepper

½ teaspoon pure chile powder, such as ancho

1½ pounds red cabbage, very thinly sliced on a mandoline (6 cups)

4 garlic cloves, thinly sliced

1. Preheat oven to 450°F.

2. Spread the pine nuts in a pie plate and toast for about 3 minutes, until golden brown.

3. On a large rimmed baking sheet, toss the brussels sprouts with 1 tablespoon olive oil and season with salt and pepper.

4. Roast for about 15 minutes, until the brussels sprouts are lightly caramelized and tender.

5. As the sprouts are caramelizing, whisk the mustard, cayenne, and chile powder in a small bowl.

6. Slowly whisk in ¼ cup olive oil and season with salt and pepper.

7. In a large bowl, toss the cabbage with the toasted pine nuts.

8. In a small skillet, heat the remaining 1 tablespoon olive oil. Add the garlic and cook over moderate heat until golden, about 1 minute.

9. Scrape the garlic and hot oil over the cabbage.

10. Add the brussels sprouts and toss, then add the dressing and toss again. Serve right away.

Baked Carrot Fries

SERVES 4

ACTIVE TIME: 20 MINUTES

TOTAL TIME: 1 HOUR AND 20 MINUTES

You will need a mandoline or food processor for this recipe. These yummy carrots give you a dose of beta-carotene in a form that's easy to swallow.

16 medium carrots, peeled and cut into 4-inch matchsticks

1 tablespoon olive oil

1 teaspoon sea salt and freshly ground black pepper to taste

½ teaspoon ground cumin (optional)

1. Preheat the oven to 425°F.

2. Place the carrot sticks in a bowl and pour the olive oil over them. Using your hands, toss the carrots in the oil to coat thoroughly.

3. Spread the carrot sticks in a single layer on a baking sheet lined with parchment paper.

4. Sprinkle with salt, pepper, and cumin (if using).

5. Bake the carrots until they begin to crisp, about 45 minutes, checking every 15 minutes or so to toss or turn the pan to ensure even cooking.

January 23
Sunday
2011

Menu

Shepherd's Pie
with Seitan and
Winter Vegetables

Flourless Chocolate Tart

—

La Spinetta Barbaresco
" Gallina
2006

Roast Cabbage and Brussel Sprouts. I love letting people know where they are sitting and what they are eating, and all the cards look nice on the table. In the background are a picture of my father and me when I was little, and one of me and Bear right after I adopted him taken by my pal Bruce Weber.

Cauliflower with Pine Nuts. I love cauliflower and this is one of my favorite recipes.

Cauliflower with Pine Nuts

SERVES 4
ACTIVE TIME: 1 HOUR
TOTAL TIME: 1 HOUR AND 30 MINUTES

Pine nuts are great with roasted cauliflower. Tomatoes make this simple roast dish even more delicious.

¼ cup extra-virgin olive oil
1 head of cauliflower, cut into florets (4 cups)
2 cups tomatoes, peeled, seeded, drained, and chopped

Pinch of red pepper flakes
¼ cup hot water
2 tablespoons pine nuts
1 garlic clove, finely chopped
2 tablespoons chopped parsley
1½ tablespoons fresh lemon juice

1. Preheat oven to 350°F.
2. In a 10- to 12-inch ovenproof skillet, heat the oil. Add the cauliflower and cook over moderately low heat, stirring, until the cauliflower starts to soften, about 10 minutes.

3. Raise the heat to moderate and cook until the cauliflower is lightly browned, about 5 minutes longer.

4. Stir in the tomatoes and red pepper flakes and cook until the tomatoes have begun to soften, about 5 minutes.

5. Add ¼ cup hot water, pine nuts, and garlic to the cauliflower.

6. Transfer the skillet to the oven and bake cauliflower for about 30 minutes, until it is very tender.

7. Stir in the parsley and lemon juice and let stand at room temperature for 30 minutes. Serve warm.

Broiled Onions with Balsamic Vinaigrette

SERVES 6

TOTAL TIME: 40 MINUTES

Red onions are sweet and a delicious addition to just about anything: burgers, sandwiches, salads. They always add a tasty touch!

2   tablespoons balsamic vinegar

1½ teaspoons chopped fresh rosemary leaves

1¾ pounds red onions (about 3 large), cut crosswise into ½-inch-thick slices

Coarse sea salt and freshly ground black pepper

¼   cup finely chopped fresh flat-leaf parsley

1. Fire up the broiler.

2. Position oven rack 4 to 6 inches from heat source. In the summer, you can prepare a medium hot charcoal or gas grill.

3. In a small saucepan, slowly heat the vinegar and rosemary until hot. Avoid letting mixture boil.

4. Remove pan from heat and let mixture stand, covered, 20 minutes.

5. Brush the onion slices on both sides with the warm oil and season with salt and pepper.

6. Grill in batches until lightly charred, 4 to 6 minutes on each side.

7. As onions finish cooking, transfer to a large bowl, separating rings.

8. While still hot, toss with vinegar mixture and parsley, and season with salt and pepper.

9. Serve warm or at room temperature.

WINTER STEWS

Winter needs a special section on stews because they are the dish of the season. You don't need an animal to make a delicious, hearty stew that sticks to your ribs. Tempeh and seitan, which Tanya Petrovna describes on page 42, will give some of these dishes the texture they need. You won't ever miss the meat.

Wake-Up Call Porridge

SERVES 1

ACTIVE TIME: 20 MINUTES

TOTAL TIME: OVERNIGHT SOAK

I wanted to include a yummy porridge for the holidays, especially good on mornings after a late night and too much celebrating.

- 2 tablespoons raw nuts, such as almonds, hazelnuts, or Brazil nuts, soaked overnight, drained, and coarsely chopped
- 1 Granny Smith apple peeled, cored, and coarsely chopped
- 2 dried white figs, coarsely chopped
- ¼ teaspoon chopped fresh ginger
- 1 teaspoon dried goji berries
- ½ teaspoon flaxseed

1. In a food processor, grind the nuts.
2. Add the apple, figs, and ginger and pulse until chunky.
3. Transfer the porridge to a bowl.
4. Top with goji berries and flaxseed.

Dal Vegetables

SERVES 8

ACTIVE TIME: 20 MINUTES

TOTAL TIME: 1 HOUR AND 20 MINUTES

Your house will smell scrumptious when you cook this hearty recipe.

- 3 tablespoons Earth Balance "butter," melted or vegetable oil
- 1 cup chopped carrots
- 1 cup peeled and cubed butternut squash
- 4 cups water
- 1 teaspoon freshly grated ginger
- 2 teaspoons turmeric
- 2 teaspoons ground coriander
- 1 teaspoon sea salt
- 1½ cups dried yellow lentils
- 2 cups broccoli florets
- 1 teaspoon brown mustard seed
- 2 teaspoons cumin seed
- 1 teaspoon fennel seed
  Brown rice, for serving

1. Add 2 tablespoons melted Earth Balance "butter," carrots, and squash to a large saucepan. Sauté for 8 minutes.
2. Add water, ginger, turmeric, coriander, salt, and lentils. Bring to a boil, then reduce heat, cover, and simmer for 1 hour.
3. Add broccoli and an additional cup of water (you can omit the water if you prefer a thicker dal), and simmer for 10 minutes.

4. While the broccoli cooks, toast the mustard, cumin, and fennel seeds in a skillet over high heat for 1 minute, or until the seeds are fragrant.

5. Add remaining Earth Balance "butter" or oil to the skillet and sauté for 1 minute.

6. Combine with the broccoli and lentil mixture, and serve with brown rice.

Seitan, Barley, and Mushroom Stew

SERVES 4

ACTIVE TIME: 30 MINUTES

TOTAL TIME: 1 HOUR AND 30 MINUTES

After this delicious stew, a nice nap in front of the fire....

2	tablespoons olive oil
3	ounces seitan, cut in 1-inch cubes
1	medium onion, finely chopped
½	celery stalk, finely chopped
4	garlic cloves, minced
12	ounces cremini mushrooms, cut into quarters
1	teaspoon dried thyme
1	teaspoon dried tarragon
1	teaspoon allspice
½	teaspoon smoked paprika
½	cup dry white wine
1	cup pearl barley
6	to 8 cups vegetable broth

Sea salt and freshly ground black pepper
Chopped fresh parsley, for garnish

1. Heat the oil in a large pot over medium heat.

2. Add the seitan and cook until browned, about 5 minutes.

3. Remove from the pot and set aside.

4. Add the onion to the same pot and cook over medium heat until softened, about 5 minutes.

5. Add the celery and garlic and cook 2 minutes, or until the garlic releases its aroma.

6. Add the mushrooms, herbs, and spices. Cook 3 to 5 minutes, or until the mushrooms begin to soften.

7. Add the reserved seitan.

8. Increase the heat to medium-high and add the wine to deglaze, scraping any bits off the bottom of the pot.

9. When the liquid reduces to one half, add the barley and broth.

10. Season with salt and pepper to taste.

11. Bring to a boil, then reduce to a simmer. Cook 50 to 60 minutes, or until the barley is tender, adding more broth if needed.

12. Taste and adjust the seasonings.

13. Serve hot, garnished with parsley.

Kale, Lentil, and Vegetable Stew

Serves 6

Total time: 55 minutes

Greens, beans, and vegetables pack this stew with powerful nutrients to keep you healthy in flu season.

2   tablespoons olive oil
1   large onion, chopped
2   large carrots, peeled and chopped (1¼ cups)
1   medium celery root (celeriac), peeled and chopped (3 cups)
1   medium rutabaga, peeled and chopped (2 cups)
    Sea salt and freshly ground pepper
1   pound brown lentils, rinsed
1   tablespoon herbes de Provence
8   cups (or more) vegetable broth
1   large bunch kale, ribs removed, leaves coarsely chopped

1. Heat oil in a large pot over high heat.
2. Add onion and carrots, celery root, and rutabaga; sprinkle with salt and pepper and sauté until beginning to soften and brown, 10 to 11 minutes.
3. Stir in lentils and herbes de Provence.
4. Add broth and kale. Reduce heat to medium-low, cover with lid slightly ajar, and simmer until lentils are tender, stirring occasionally, about 20 minutes. Add more broth to thin, if desired.
5. Season with salt and pepper and serve.

Seitan Chili

Serves 4

Active time: 30 minutes

Total time: 1 hour

Serve with garlic bread. Make this chili the day before and freeze some extra.

1   tablespoon olive oil
1   large onion, chopped
1   jalapeño, seeded and minced
4   garlic cloves, minced
1   pound seitan, cut into ½-inch dice
2   tablespoons chili powder
1   tablespoon ground cumin
1   teaspoon dried oregano
1   (28-ounce) can whole plum tomatoes, with liquid
1   (15-ounce) can fire-roasted tomatoes with chiles, with liquid
1½ cups cooked or 1 (15-ounce) can black beans, rinsed and drained
1½ cups cooked or 1 (15-ounce) can red kidney beans, rinsed and drained
1   tablespoon minced chipotle chile in adobo
    Sea salt and freshly ground black pepper
1   to 2 cups vegetable broth

1. Heat the oil in a large pot over medium heat.
2. Add the onion and jalapeño. Cook, stirring, for 5 minutes, or until softened.
3. Add the garlic, seitan, and spices. Cook until the seitan is browned, about 5 minutes.

4. While the plum tomatoes are still in the can, use a knife to break them up a bit.

5. Add the tomatoes, beans, and chipotle to seitan mixture. Season with salt and pepper to taste, and stir to combine. Add broth for desired consistency.

6. Bring stew to a boil then reduce to a simmer for 30 minutes or longer to blend the flavors.

7. Serve hot.

Mushroom, Barley, and Squash Stew

Serves 4
Total time: 45–50 minutes

This is better than beef stew—and takes less time to make.

- 3 cups brown or cremini mushrooms
- 3 cups oyster mushrooms
- 2 cups coarsely chopped onions
- 2-4 garlic cloves, minced or pressed
- 2 teaspoons vegetable oil
- 2 teaspoons dried dill (1 tablespoon fresh)
- 1 teaspoon dried thyme
- 1 butternut or other winter squash, peeled, seeded, and cubed (about 6 cups)
- 2 cups water or vegetable stock
- 2 cups fresh or frozen corn kernels
- 2 cups cooked or 1 (15-ounce) can kidney beans, rinsed and drained
- 2 tablespoons apple cider vinegar
- Sea salt and freshly ground black pepper to taste
- 1 tablespoon cornmeal

1. Wash the mushrooms with as little water as possible.

2. Quarter the brown mushrooms.

3. Trim the bottoms of the oyster mushroom clumps and gently pull them apart into smaller, bite-size clusters. Set aside.

4. In a covered soup pot on low heat, sauté the onions and garlic in the oil, stirring often, until the onions are translucent. Add the dill and thyme, and cook for 2 minutes, stirring continuously. Add the squash, brown mushrooms, and water or stock, and bring to a boil. Simmer until the squash is tender, about 3 to 5 minutes. Stir in the corn and beans. When the stew returns to a simmer, add the oyster mushrooms, vinegar, and salt and pepper to taste. Stir in the cornmeal and simmer, stirring often, until the broth is thickened.

Gingerbread

SERVES 8

TOTAL TIME: 55 MINUTES

Gingerbread is a holiday must.

1 cup Earth Balance "butter"

1 cup cane sugar

2 teaspoons grated fresh ginger

½ cup molasses

½ cup warm water

2½ cups whole wheat pastry flour

1 tablespoon baking soda

½ teaspoon salt

2 teaspoons powdered ginger

1. Preheat the oven to 350°F.

2. Cut an 8-inch round of wax or parchment paper. Grease and flour the side and bottom an 8-inch round cake pan and fit the prepared paper in the bottom.

3. In a large bowl, beat the Earth Balance "butter," sugar, and fresh ginger together until the mixture is light.

4. In a separate small bowl, mix the molasses with ½ cup warm water.

5. In another bowl, mix the flour, baking soda, salt, and powdered ginger together.

6. Add the molasses mixture to the Earth Balance "butter"-and-sugar mixture.

7. Add the flour mixture and stir just until the ingredients are blended but with no large lumps.

8. Pour the batter into the prepared pan and bake for 35 minutes, or until a toothpick comes out clean.

9. Allow the gingerbread to cool in the pan and invert to remove.

Crepes

Serves 4
Total time: 20 minutes

Crepes are always a huge hit. You won't see them served that much anymore. So do it—don't be scared! They are no harder than pancakes.

1½ cups whole wheat flour
 ½ teaspoon sea salt
 1 tablespoon tapioca flour or arrowroot
2½ cups water
 1 tablespoon canola oil, plus extra for cooking
    Earth Balance "butter"
    Cane sugar

1. Heat your crepe or sauté pan over medium heat.
2. Sift the flour, salt, and tapioca flour through a fine-mesh strainer or sifter into a large bowl. Whisk together.
3. Add the water and oil, and whisk again until well combined.
4. If you are using a nonstick pan, use only a very light coating of oil. Ideally, use a pastry brush to spread out a very small drop of oil.
5. Use a ⅓-cup measuring cup to scoop the batter.
6. Hold the pan at a 45-degree angle, pour in the batter at the top of the pan, and quickly swirl the pan in a circular motion to spread out the batter into a very thin layer. Adjust the amount of batter to suit the size of the pan you are using. The crepes should be very, very thin.
7. Cook for about 3 minutes on the first side, or until bubbles appear over the whole crepe. Flip and cook for about 1 more minute.
8. Fold the crepe in half, then in half again. Lay it on a plate or baking tray while you work on the others.
9. Serve immediately with a generous helping of Earth Balance "butter" or cane sugar. Or serve with the Strawberry-Rhubarb Crepe Filling below.

Strawberry Rhubarb Crepe Filling

Serves 10
Total time: 5 minutes

Here is a yummy filling!

1 cup frozen strawberries, thawed
1 cup frozen rhubarb, thawed
¼ cup agave
   Pinch of sea salt
4 cups banana, cut into half-moons

1. Blend the strawberries, rhubarb, agave and salt until smooth.
2. Either fill the middle of a crepe with some sliced bananas and about 2 tablespoons of the sauce, or just top the crepes with both the bananas and the sauce and enjoy.

Ice Cream Bombe

SERVES 8
ACTIVE TIME: 20 MINUTES
TOTAL TIME: 35 MINUTES

I love to use an old tin mold. It's not that much trouble to make an ice cream bombe, and it's so much more festive than a scoop of ice cream. All you need is a mold, which you can pick up anywhere or order online. You can use dairy-free vanilla ice cream. When I was growing up we had a wonderful chef who used to make this. I loved seeing the ice cream come out of the mold and be garnished with chocolate or fruit.

 1   gallon dairy-free ice cream
     Shaved dark chocolate or berries or both

1. Remove the ice cream from the freezer and mix in a bowl to soften, about 10 minutes.
2. Press ice cream into the mold, stopping an inch or two from the top.
3. Shave in dark chocolate or add a layer of berries.
4. Cover with remaining ice cream.
5. Put in freezer until frozen solid, about 2 hours.
6. Hold mold under hot water for a few seconds and invert onto a plate.
7. Remove mold from ice cream and sprinkle bombe with shaved dark chocolate.

Apple Cinnamon Bars

SERVES 14
ACTIVE TIME: 15 MINUTES
TOTAL TIME: 1 HOUR AND 15 MINUTES

These delicious bars are a great grab-and-go snack.

 2   cups organic unsweetened almond milk
1½   cups organic steel-cut oats
 ½   cup chopped pecans
 ½   cup raisins
 ½   cup ground flaxseeds
 2   teaspoons vanilla extract
1½   teaspoons ground cinnamon
 2   Pink Lady apples, cored and grated

1. Preheat oven to 350°F.
2. Mix all ingredients together in a large bowl.
3. Transfer to a foil– or parchment paper–lined 9-inch square baking pan; press down mixture and smooth out the top.
4. Bake until firm and golden brown, about 1 hour.
5. Let cool in pan.
6. Cut into squares and serve warm or at room temperature.

Peanut Butter and Jelly Cups

MAKES 50
TOTAL TIME: 1 HOUR AND 45 MINUTES

Who doesn't love PB&J? And with the added benefits of dark chocolate?

PEANUT BUTTER FILLING:

7½ ounces dairy-free white chocolate, chopped
¼ cup Earth Balance "butter"
¾ cup peanut butter
1 teaspoon sea salt

CHOCOLATE CUPS:

1½ pounds bittersweet dairy-free chocolate, chopped and tempered. Most high-quality chocolate is already tempered. Check the label, because the process is complicated.
50 (1¼-inch-wide), sturdy foil cups
⅔ cup seedless raspberry jam or currant or grape jelly
Sea salt, for garnish

FOR THE FILLING:

1. In a small saucepan, melt chocolate in Earth Balance "butter."
2. Stir in the peanut butter and salt.
3. Transfer the filling to a piping bag fitted with a medium tip

FOR THE CHOCOLATE CUPS:

1. Spoon the tempered chocolate mixture into a piping bag fitted with a small tip.
2. Line a baking sheet with parchment paper.
3. Set half the foil cups on the sheet and fill them with chocolate. Tilt the cups to coat them completely, then pour the excess chocolate into a bowl.
4. Turn the coated cups upside down on the baking sheet and let stand for 30 seconds.
5. Turn the cups right side up and let stand until the chocolate is firm, about 10 minutes.
6. Repeat to make the remaining chocolate cups.

FINISH THE CUPS:

1. Half-fill the cups with the peanut butter.
2. Spoon a rounded ½ teaspoon jam over the peanut butter.
3. Pipe chocolate on top of the jam
4. Tap gently to level the chocolate.
5. Top with a few flakes of sea salt.
6. Let stand until set, about 15 minutes.

Ice Cream Bombe. The little critters I got in Merano, Italy at their Christmas fair. They are made from bark.

RESOURCES

PRODUCTS

Earth Balance
www.earthbalancenatural.com
A delicious butter alternative.

So Delicious
www.turtlemountain.com
Amazing coconut milk.

Vegenaise
www.followyourheart.com
Instead of mayonnaise
use Vegenaise.

Fine and Raw Chocolate
www.fineandraw.com

Endangered Species Chocolate
www.chocolatebar.com

Fearless Chocolate
www.fearlesschocolate.com
I love chocolate, need I say more?

Julian Bakery
www.julianbakery.com
A great source for gluten-free
and low-carb breads. They ship
nationwide.

Organic Avenue
www.organicavenue.com
Organic Avenue has great juices,
raw foods, and chocolate.

Mayzan Swami Nathan
www.mayzing.com
Delicious meatless meat!

Gaiam
www.gaiam.com
Great organic products,
including sheets.

Liquiteria
www.liquiteria.com
A source for delicious juices.

Objets d'Art & Spirit
www.objetsdartandspirit.com
My go-to store for the best
presents, oils, bubble baths—
you name it, Kirpal has it!

Claudio Cova
www.pastashop-merano.com
Delicious grain pasta of
every kind.

PEOPLE AND PLACES

Cornelia Guest
www.CorneliaGuest.com
Find out about my world.

Bruce Weber
www.bruceweber.com

Joanna Vargas
www.joannavargas.com

Jeff DePeron
www.huraathletics.com

Dr. Michael Galitzer
www.ahealth.com

Tanya Petrovna
www.nativefoods.com

Richard Brown,
Amagansett Wine and Spirits
www.amagensettwine.com

Chef Michael Guerrieri
www.citysandwichnyc.com
and *www.chefguerrieri.com*

Pauline Esposito, Ph.D.
www.awakeningofthesoul.com and
www.seraphim12foundation.com
Pauline is a wonderful and
gifted healer.

Dr. Richard Palmquist
www.lovapet.com
Dr. Palmquist's Holistic Resource
List for Pet Owners
1. Find a holistic veterinarian.
   www.ahvma.org
2. Support research into
   complementary, alternative,
   and integrative veterinary
   medicine.
   www.foundation.ahvma.org
3. Poison control
   *www.aspca.org/pet-care/
   poison-control/*
4. EPA pet flea product safety
   *www.epa.gov/opp00001/
   health/petproductseval.html*
5. Allergic reactions to vaccines
   and how to report a reaction
   *www.veterinarypartner.com/
   Content.plx?P=A&A=527*
6. My favorite veterinary
   nutritionist
   www.susanwynn.com
7. My favorite holistic
   veterinary radio show,
   "Ask Martha's Vet with
   Dr. Marty Goldstein,"
   Mondays, 8 PM EST
   *www.drmarty.com/
   integrativemedicine.htm*
8. My favorite pet magazine
   *www.animalwellness
   magazine.com/index.php*
9. Animal health and safety
   recalls *www.fda.gov/Safety/
   Recalls/default.htm*
10. Environmental toxins
    information
    *http://library.med.utah.edu/
    ed/eduservices/handouts/
    Toxins_Web/toxin-urls.html*
11. To learn more about USDA-
    recommended nutrients

*www.fda.gov/food/labeling
nutrition/consumer
information/ucm078889.htm*

12. Dietary supplements
*www.nutrition.gov/
nal_display/index.php?info_
center=11&tax_level=1&tax_
subject=393*

Dr. Deborah Kleinman
Cindrich 516-883-1305;
www.sandyhollowchiropractic.com
and *www.10thstreetchiropractic.com*
Craniosacral chiropractor and
homeopath.

Peri Lyons
www.perilyons.com and
www.perilyonsintuitive.com
Peri's views on the world are fun,
intelligent, and always give you
a fascinating new way of looking
at things.

Chowhound
www.chowhound.chow.com/boards
The best place to find restaurants
all over the world.

The Dream Spa
www.lighthealthresearch.com
My friend Mellon Thomas created
the Dream Spa. I find light therapy
to be incredibly healing.

Henri Chenot
www.henrichenot.com
Henri Chenot and his wife
Dominique have an incredible
wellness center.

Ted Hope
www.blogs.indiewire.com/tedhope
www.hopeforfilm.com
www.hammertonail.com
www.bowlofnoses.hopeforfilm.com
Great insight on films and life.

Gordon VeneKlasen VW
(VeneKlasen/Werner) in Berlin
www.vwberlin.com
Michael Werner Gallery
in New York
www.michaelwerner.com
My darling Gordon VeneKlasen
has the most wonderful artists
and galleries and the best info
on the art world.

Janet Hranicky, Ph.D.
www.ahealth.com and
www.HranickyPsychoOncology.com
Brilliant on health issues.

The Well Daily
www.thewelldaily.com
A great guide for a
wholesome lifestyle.

Greta Guide
www.gretaguide.com
All the newest ideas.

CHARITIES

Humane Society of New York
www.humanesocietyny.org

Farm Sanctuary
www.farmsanctuary.org

PETA
www.peta.org

Gentle Giants Rescue—
Burt and Tracy Ward
www.gentlegiantsrescue.com
My beloved Bear came from here.

Animal Rescue Site
www.theanimalrescuesite.com

Thoroughbred Retirement
Foundation
www.trfinc.org

Elephant Nature Park
www.elephantnaturepark.org

Performing Animal Welfare
Society (PAWS)
www.pawsweb.org

The Breast Cancer Site
www.thebreastcancersite.com

Best Buddies
www.bestbuddies.org
Great way to help others.

Green Chimneys
www.greenchimneys.org
Kids and critters—what could
be better?

Partners in Health
www.pih.org

Friends of Nan Bush and
Palomino Fund at Colorado
State University
*http://csuvth.colostate.edu/
diagnostic_and_support/
administration/low_income_
assistance.aspx*

Veterinary Teaching Hospital
www.csuvth.colostate.edu

Elephant Family
www.elephantfamily.org

METRIC CONVERSIONS

The recipes in this book have not been tested with metric measurements, so some variations might occur.

Remember that the weight of dry ingredients varies according to the volume or density factor: 1 cup of flour weighs far less than 1 cup of sugar, and 1 tablespoon doesn't necessarily hold 3 teaspoons.

General Formula for Metric Conversion

Ounces to grams	multiply ounces by 28.35
Grams to ounces	multiply ounces by 0.035
Pounds to grams	multiply pounds by 453.5
Pounds to kilograms	multiply pounds by 0.45
Cups to liters	multiply cups by 0.24
Fahrenheit to Celsius	subtract 32 from Fahrenheit temperature, multiply by 5, divide by 9
Celsius to Fahrenheit	multiply Celsius temperature by 9, divide by 5, add 32

Volume (Liquid) Measurements

1 teaspoon = ⅙ fluid ounce = 5 milliliters
1 tablespoon = ½ fluid ounce = 15 milliliters
2 tablespoons = 1 fluid ounce = 30 milliliters
¼ cup = 2 fluid ounces = 60 milliliters
⅓ cup = 2 ⅔ fluid ounces = 79 milliliters
½ cup = 4 fluid ounces = 118 milliliters
1 cup or ½ pint = 8 fluid ounces = 250 milliliters
2 cups or 1 pint = 16 fluid ounces = 500 milliliters
4 cups or 1 quart = 32 fluid ounces = 1,000 milliliters
1 gallon = 4 liters

Volume (Dry) Measurements

¼ teaspoon = 1 milliliter
½ teaspoon = 2 milliliters
¾ teaspoon = 4 milliliters
1 teaspoon = 5 milliliters
1 tablespoon = 15 milliliters
¼ cup = 59 milliliters
⅓ cup = 79 milliliters
½ cup = 118 milliliters
⅔ cup = 158 milliliters
¾ cup = 177 milliliters
1 cup = 225 milliliters
4 cups or 1 quart = 1 liter
½ gallon = 2 liters
1 gallon = 4 liters

Weight (Mass) Measurements

1 ounce = 30 grams
2 ounces = 55 grams
3 ounces = 85 grams
4 ounces = ¼ pound = 125 grams
8 ounces = ½ pound = 240 grams
12 ounces = ¾ pound = 375 grams
16 ounces = 1 pound = 454 grams

Linear Measurements

½ in = 1 ½ cm
1 inch = 2 ½ cm
6 inches = 15 cm
8 inches = 20 cm
10 inches = 25 cm
12 inches = 30 cm
20 inches = 50 cm

Oven Temperature Equivalents, Fahrenheit (F) and Celsius (C)

100°F = 38°C
200°F = 95°C
250°F = 120°C
300°F = 150°C
350°F = 180°C
400°F = 205°C
450°F = 230° C

INDEX